PRAISE FOR PAWS & EFFECT

"This gem of a book confirms what I already feel: that my bond with my dog is deep, and aids the collective health of my family. *Paws & Effect* is a must-read!"

—David Mizejewski, host of
Backyard Habitat on Animal Planet

"What I loved was that the book showed you the all-stars of the canine world, and then ordinary dogs who do extraordinary things every day, like my dogs. Dogs detect cancer, warn about seizures, relieve pain, and tirelessly visit the sick. Aren't dogs amazing? *Paws & Effect* by Sharon Sakson certainly proves that they are."

—Sue Simmons, WNBC News

"The idea that dogs can assist blind and deaf people is well known, however it is also true that dogs can detect cancer, alert to oncoming seizures, reduce psychological stress, help cope with depression, and even keep people with coronary heart problems alive longer. In a series of interesting, informative, and often poignant stories about real people, Sharon Sakson tells you about how dogs help to heal the mind and the body. After reading *Paws & Effect*, you may well start feeling that having a dog at home is like having a special kind of doctor in your house."

—Stanley Coren, author of *How Dogs Think*,
The Intelligence of Dogs, and many other books

Paws & Effect

THE HEALING POWER OF DOGS

SHARON SAKSON

FOREWORD BY **DAVID FREI,**
CO-HOST, "THE WESTMINSTER KENNEL
CLUB DOG SHOW," USA NETWORK

alyson books
NEW YORK

Manufactured in THE UNITED STATES OF AMERICA.

Published by
ALYSON BOOKS
245 WEST 17TH STREET
NEW YORK, NEW YORK 10011

Distribution in the United Kingdom by
TURNAROUND PUBLISHER SERVICES LTD.
UNIT 3, OLYMPIA TRADING ESTATE
COBURG ROAD, WOOD GREEN
LONDON N22 6TZ ENGLAND

First Edition: DECEMBER 2007

07 08 09 10 **a** 10 9 8 7 6 5 4 3 2 1

ISBN 1-59350-038-6
ISBN-13 978-1-59350-038-2
LIBRARY OF CONGRESS CATALOGING-IN PUBLICATION DATA ARE ON FILE.

Book design by VICTOR MINGOVITS

"When man is in trouble, God sends him a dog."
— ALPHONSE DE LAMARTINE (1790–1869)

To *Abby*, my lovely *Whippet*, who shared my life
for *seventeen and a half* wonderful years.
Until we meet again.

CONTENTS

FOREWORD

by David Frei

Co-host, *"Westminster Kennel Club Dog Show,"*
USA Network

IN MY WORK as the national spokesperson for Delta Society and as president of Angel On A Leash (a charity of the Westminster Kennel Club), I have personally seen thousands of very special people living wonderful stories every day as a result of their direct contact with the healing power of dogs.

Through agencies such as Delta Society, the Good Dog Foundation, Therapy Dogs International, and, recently, Angel On A Leash, the numbers of active service and therapy dogs continue to rise in an expanding variety of settings. Their missions-in-common, about which their leaders and volunteers are passionate, are improving human health and quality of life through the human-animal bond.

As Sharon Sakson shows us in *Paws and Effect*, the roles of therapy and service dogs often overlap as both helpers and healers of their human charges, and the results can be amazing!

I saw this for myself through witnessing the experience

of a man named Mike Lingenfelter, a type-A personality, who had been left with extensive heart damage and unstable angina after emergency open-heart surgery. I first met Mike ten years ago when he was chosen as a "Beyond Limits" Delta Society Award winner. Years earlier, he had been talked into getting a "therapy" dog by his psychiatrist and his cardiologist to help him deal with his suicidal depression and made him get much needed exercise. Reluctant at first, Mike eventually got into animal-assisted therapy in a serious way with a Golden Retriever named Dakota (the dog himself a rescue with a heart problem). Within months, Mike found life worth living again, even though he was dealing with crippling angina attacks every few weeks.

Then, amazingly, Dakota learned to sense when Mike was about to have a heart crisis. He would alert Mike that the crisis was coming before Mike could feel it himself, and this allowed Mike to take his medication early enough to head off the worst of the effects. As Mike's protector, Dakota saved his life many times with this alerting behavior, and this allowed Mike to return to the workforce, with Dakota acting as his service dog. (That's just part of the incredible story, which became the subject of a book Mike and I co-wrote: *The Angel by My Side*, named Book of the Year in 2003 by the Dog Writers Association of America.)

Sharon's research for *Paws and Effect* took her to academic institutions, veterinarians' offices, dog breeders, charitable organizations, and even the military, wherein she discovered documentation for what so many of us understand (and what Delta Society has been telling everyone for the last thirty years!): that the loving presence of a dog can avert, and transport us through, grave illness, whether physical or psychological.

But even more important, Sharon's investigation took her deep into the hearts and lives of dogs and their owners.

My friend and colleague Mike Lingenfelter said of his beloved Dakota: "He didn't just help me—I know many people who met

Dakota and were blessed by him and had their lives changed forever . . . Dakota has presented to the world the power of the human-animal bond and the lesson that God's four-legged creatures have special powers—if we'd just take the time to listen and try to understand them."

As author Sharon Sakson makes clear in *Paws and Effect*, dogs are not only faithful and intuitive companions, but also, on a deeper level, spiritual guides, who, in their resilience, intelligence, affability, courage, and perseverance, both model and support healthy living.

For thousands of years, dogs were bred to do specific jobs for their humans—guarding the flocks, moving livestock from one place to another, helping hunters bring home dinner for the family, pulling carts, ridding the home and farm of pests and vermin, or even serving as a foot warmer in bed.

The Industrial Revolution eliminated a lot of those jobs in the eighteenth and nineteenth centuries, as machinery was created to do a lot of those jobs. Suddenly, the dogs were out of work. But that was okay; they were now being bred mostly for companionship instead of performance.

But what made it even more okay was when we humans figured out that we could provide them with another job: taking care of us.

In the end, here is what it comes down to: We should worry less about what we teach our dogs, and more about what we learn from them.

—September 2007

INTRODUCTION

IN 2006, A BOOK ABOUT DOGS that a friend and I created landed on various top-seller lists in many bookstores and on the Internet. *Paws and Reflect: A Special Bond Between Man and Dog* was written to entertain a small audience of dog-loving men, their friends and families, but it turned out that all kinds of dog lovers were buying the book: gay and straight, young and elderly, people who liked mysteries and funny stories, who showed dogs professionally and as amateurs, cat fanciers, bird aficionados, breeders of pygmy pigs, and occasionally even someone who claimed they didn't really care for dogs at all, but who were just drawn to the book and loved reading it.

After only two months on the market, all copies of the book were sold, and it went into a second printing. Around that time, I tried to figure out the reasons that made people buy copies for their friends and recommend it to their acquaintances.

The book, in which men talked about the relationships with their dogs, has various themes. Some men said their dogs were their family. Others said they were trusted, supportive friends. Still others talked about instinctive, primal connections to their canines. But as I perused the stories, another theme emerged, one neither of us had thought of before.

It was not the theme of how rewarding and mutually satisfying the love between a man and his dog can be; that's a well-known facet of dog ownership. Instead, there was evidence throughout the book that the dogs had some understanding of what was wrong with each owner, or of what was missing, or of what needed healing. In the stories the men told, it was not just they who sought out the dogs and felt enriched by loving and nurturing them. The dogs themselves had taken on an active role in many of the stories, promoting the bond between themselves and their respective humans. The dogs were reaching out, not just to understand their people, but also to be of help.

This idea came through most clearly in the stories of men who were ill. Two men who lived with life-threatening illnesses felt their dogs had taught them lessons in perseverance and acceptance. Other men talked about how their dogs took away some of their grief—over the loss of a parent, a partner or a career. Men with depression said their dogs comforted them and refused to let them mope around in despair. The dogs taught their owners by their example to find joy in whatever pleasures life holds, whether a baked-liver dog biscuit or a warm spot in the sun. One after another, the dogs in the book didn't just bond with their humans; they healed their humans.

Dogs have always helped people. They have herded our sheep, chased predators from our homes, given us unconditional love. But the emotional and spiritual support the men of *Paws and Reflect* received from their dogs seemed like a new and different kind of help. To understand if this was merely my perception or an evolution in the human-canine relationship, I began to research these ideas. I wanted to know if helping us in ways that were not only physical, but emotional and spiritual as well, was a modern adaptation to life with humans. Had we always relied on dogs to support us with their presence and to help us reach life-affirming goals, such as the will to recover from an illness, a setback, or a major depression? Or was there something new in the human-canine relationship?

My research led me to academic institutions, veterinarians' offices, dog breeders, and charitable organizations such as Pets Are Wonderful Support, Canine Companions for Independence, and Assistance Dogs Institute. What I discovered was that the presence of dogs was altering the course of human life for many, many people, in ways that were sometimes practical, as with a Seeing Eye or hearing dog, and sometimes seemingly mystical and mysterious, as with alert dogs and therapy dogs and social work dogs. Humans have always kept dogs nearby, watchful for possible danger. But now dogs are also alerting their humans that an epileptic seizure might be imminent. Dogs are calming autistic children and bringing back pleasant memories for Alzheimer's patients, or assisting in the physical therapy of toddlers and giving little sons and daughters the courage to testify against their abusers. Police departments have long used dogs for guard and attack work. But now, police depend on them to find hidden nitrogen, cocaine, guns, and cadavers. Dogs are now working in hospitals, nursing homes, mental institutions, rehab facilities, and prisons.

In this century, humankind has found many ways to employ the healing power of dogs. The dogs, in their forbearance, have offered their cooperation. Everywhere my research took me there were large dogs, tiny dogs, calm dogs, hyper dogs, well-trained dogs, and instinctual dogs, all of them doing their best to partner their human friend. My heart was, and remains, touched by their vigilance and steadfast service. All my wide-ranging research reinforced one fact: that the bond between our dogs and us enriches our world. They honor us by their friendship. They offer us their lives.

CHAPTER 1

LIVING WITH HEALING DOGS

WHEN I TRACE BACK my interest in the healing power of dogs, I have to start at the beginning, which takes me back to age twelve. In that year, my mother took to bed with an unexplained illness. Because I was in seventh grade, breezy, confident, and wise, I assumed she had a lingering case of flu and sighed with annoyance whenever she asked me to look after my three younger siblings.

Our relatives and friends said, "Your mother will be better soon," and I believed them, the way a child would. Instead, over the next months, the situation deteriorated. There were fewer and fewer days when my mother felt well enough to get up and help us with homework. Finally, one warm May afternoon, we arrived home to the sight of an ambulance in the driveway, and just beyond it, parked askew, our father's car.

My brother, Johnny, and I ran into our house, where we

saw the even stranger sight of our father descending the staircase, carrying our mother.

He had never carried her before. He often complained that she was too heavy, that her clothes were too tight, that if firemen ever came to our house to rescue us, they wouldn't be able to get her out. It wasn't true; she was a petite 5 foot, 1 inch and 105 pounds. He amused himself by playing on her anxieties about how she looked. Yet now here he was, carrying her in his arms. She looked frail and small. He laid her on the gurney and the ambulance workers strapped her in.

Our father told us she was going to the hospital because she needed more treatment and it would be better for her to get it there. She would get better in the hospital, and then she would come home. He sounded very certain, so we were reassured.

It was a confusing time. In an excess of sympathy and caring, no one wanted her children to know that she was dying. Instead, they continuously tried to cheer us up. Their strategies worked because we had been trained to believe what adults said.

The next day, our maternal grandmother, Kay, took us to Robert's Pet Shop, on a corner of Warren Avenue near her apartment in Trenton, New Jersey. We needed food for Johnny's two turtles and some pebbles and a fancy castle for Sandy's goldfish. My pet had been a dog, a mutt named Shadow who resembled a black Golden Retriever. He was born in the stable where I took riding lessons, and while we loved him, he developed a troubling habit of attacking the men who did the gardening for the homes on our block. Our yard was not fenced. Shadow stayed near us, watching baseball or jump rope or hide-and-seek with one eye while he warmed himself in the sun. But the minute a gardener appeared in any of the adjoining yards, he flew off the property and not only barked but sank his teeth into the legs of any of the men he could get near.

We knew why. When he was only a year old, he had followed

us across the Robinettes' lawn and onto the Mersons' property, where we took a path toward the back alley and planned to proceed to the home of the Hughes' children. We were a long stream of neighborhood kids. A gardener appeared in the door of the Mersons' garage, a hoe in his hand. With no provocation at all, he stepped out and smacked Shadow in the head. Shadow fell to the ground, unconscious. I was hysterical; Johnny thought he was dead; one of the Hughes boys, Brian, picked up Shadow and carried him back to our house. Shadow recovered, but he never forgot. From that moment on, he hated all gardeners. This event changed him from a calm, compliant dog to a dog who became a threatening monster on the several days a week gardeners were present. We were supposed to keep him in the house in the afternoon. We never remembered. Eventually, Mommy explained to us that Shadow was going to have to go out to the country and live at our grandparents' farm, where hopefully he would never see another gardener again.

In the cool glow from Robert's lighted aquariums, I exhumed a copy of *Dog World* magazine from a book rack. A Wire Fox Terrier graced the cover, and his beauty and stature took my breath away. Turning the pages, I fell totally under the spell of purebred dogs. Pointers and Chesapeake Bay Retrievers, Greyhounds and Bassets, Bernese Mountain Dogs and Great Danes and Chihuahuas and Collies and Corgis. All these dogs amazed and enchanted me. With this magazine in hand, I was able to put aside the thought of our mother, hooked to oxygen and intravenous fluids in the hospital, and think about something else. In that split second in the pet shop, a future opened before me that I had not contemplated, a future filled with beautiful dogs. I would be the one holding the well-groomed Standard Poodle on the thin show lead, smiling as we accepted the Best in Show trophy.

My father was cold, distant, and preoccupied, but he was roused by my insistent prodding to drive us to Merrybrook Kennels in

Long Valley, New Jersey, where I chose a Wire Fox terrier with the guidance of the great breeder Mrs. Franklin Koehler. I didn't know it at the time, but she was a pillar in the breed and would become my first mentor. It was amazing that my father, so cheap in many ways, agreed to shell out the whopping $350 price of a purebred dog. He was not inclined to be so generous when it came to Dolly's housing arrangements. He put up a makeshift fence that he assumed would hold an active, eager terrier puppy during the hours I was at school. He was wrong. Dolly escaped, and only two weeks into our partnership, she was struck and killed by a car.

While I was interviewing men for my book *Paws & Reflect*, several of them mentioned that they saw the deaths of their childhood dogs as lessons in the impermanence of physical life and the permeating quality of love. If Dolly's death was supposed to be a lesson for me, I missed it. I was already depressed about my mother's absence. When Dolly died, I took to bed and was unable to get up. My father returned to Mrs. Koehler for a second puppy, Bonnie, who was granted permission to stay in the house when I wasn't with her in order to avoid the fate of her predecessor.

If someone asked me now which breed would be best at consoling a child over the loss of her mother, a Wire Fox Terrier would be low on my list. Bonnie did not like to sit still. She would absorb only a few minutes of hugs and kisses before demanding to be set free. She was always busy chasing small animals or barking at passersby. Like most terriers, she abstained from making direct eye contact. But when my mother died, Bonnie was the only physical being who offered me any kind of comfort. She didn't lower her standards because of my grief and allow me more cuddle time. She just made it clear that she didn't see the point. There was a big world out there to explore. When the leash was snapped to her collar, we walked endlessly through Cadwalder Park. Down to the freezing cold creek where she lapped a drink while I hopped from rock to rock. Across to the playground, where she refused to ride the swings or the wheel but let me push her down the sliding board. Into the bushes behind Kathy McCormack's house, where we spied on my best friend and her family.

In the weeks after my mother's death, no one noticed us passing through the house like ghosts. Everyone was consumed inside by his or her own grief. I wanted to shut the door of my bedroom and never come out again, but I couldn't do that because of Bonnie. She felt like my heart, the only part of me that carried on. She was unfailingly lively, cute, sweet, and beautiful in my eyes. I had to carry on with my life because she did.

The black depression of my mother's death settled over me like a cloud and many, many nights I decided that the only way out was to die. I spent a lot of time considering various methods of suicide. Would the gun in my father's bedroom closet go off if I put it to my head? How many Valium pills would you have to consume to make sure you died and didn't just turn into a vegetable? What about jumping off the roof of the house? The problem with all the methods was the absence of a guarantee that they would work. And there was one lingering detail: There would be no one to take care of Bonnie. No one in the family felt about her the way I did. There is a dose of genetic material that separates a dog lover from a non-dog lover and no amount of explaining can ever cross the divide. Bonnie was the sole reason I never pressed the razor blade to my wrists or dropped in front of a speeding train. She needed me when no one else did.

It was not apparent to me then that I was witnessing the healing power that a dog can bring to a person's life. If I thought about it at all, it was the other way around. I was devoting my life to make her happy. It took the distance of adulthood to see the truth; Bonnie kept me on this earth. She didn't heal me, but she provided the possibility that I would still be alive to be healed some day. Her presence was the antidote that defused the pain of petty insults from other children and all the times I was forgotten by my father. She comforted me with her wild spirit, but often it was her physical nearness I craved. My father was proud of his German heritage. He aligned himself with the concept of Prussian military toughness. When people feel sympathy, they like to take your hand, squeeze your shoulder, and stroke your arm. My father despised all of those things. His co-workers, the doctors and nurses and physical therapists and lab technicians, even the telephone operators and television repairmen and girls who delivered the flowers; all of them would have known about the death of his wife and want to offer sympathy. It was probably hard enough to say 'Thank you' and push the grief away all day. He did not want to be confronted with it in the evenings, in his own home. He rebuffed any attempt to touch or hug me. The healing power of another being pressed against your skin came only from Bonnie.

We moved to a sterile new home in Pennsylvania, and I enrolled in a strange new school where sports stars and cheerleaders were the only honored students. All others walked in their shadows.

My father let me get a second dog. Woody was another Wire Fox Terrier, a show dog who had grown just a little too big for the ring. Bonnie joyously welcomed the presence of another of her species. Gram decided to buy me a Saint Bernard, a generous gesture on her part because she had always loved the breed.

These three dogs greeted me every day with wagging tails and kissing tongues. They loved me enthusiastically and didn't care at all about the heavy grief I carried around inside.

Trenton had one of the largest and grandest dog shows in the country. On the grounds of the Lawrenceville Armory, I walked past elegant Greyhounds, highly brushed Collies, yapping Chihuahuas, funny Dachshunds, and felt strangely at home.

My father had no feeling for dogs. He protested that he liked them, but what he liked was a vision of a robotically obedient dog confined behind a fence. He didn't like interaction with animals. I liked dogs with soft noses and pleading eyes. I liked their mischievousness and their willingness to submit. I liked training dogs and helping them figure things out. I liked hugging them and snuggling with them. I liked their clarity. If they loved you, they gave you everything. When they were unhappy, they lay in a corner. They never held a grudge nor dwelt on past mistakes. They didn't pretend to like you; they either liked you or they didn't. There was no gray area. Everything was the present. Their lives were both pure and simple.

When you say you owe your life to your dogs, people assume you are speaking rhetorically. But I'm not. For me, it's a fact.

In the past fifteen years, scientists the world over have established beyond doubt the therapeutic value of dogs. An American study of ninety two patients hospitalized in coronary care units for angina or heart attack found that those who owned pets were more likely to be alive a year later than those who did not. Twenty-eight percent of those who did not own pets died during that time. Only 6 percent of patients who owned pets died within a year. They must have felt as I did, that taking care of your pet is an important responsibility. You can't count on anyone else to do it. You've got to show up every day.

Researchers at University of California–Davis documented that people with pets were approached more often for conversation than when they were alone; blind and wheelchair-bound children with their guide dogs in public places were approached for social contact ten times more frequently than when they were without their dogs.

In England, Cambridge researchers discovered that within a month of taking a cat or dog into their home, new owners reported a highly significant reduction in minor ailments. At

Warwick University, a study found that people who were poor at making friends, confiding in others, and showing love were able to lavish affection on a pet.

A Japanese Animal Hospital Association study of people over sixty-five found that pet owners made 30 percent fewer visits to doctors than those who had no pet.

At the Baker Medical Research Institute in Melbourne, Australia, a study of some 6,000 patients revealed that those with pets had lower blood pressure, a lower cholesterol level, and as a result, a diminished risk of heart attack.

Experts say that at least part of the reason is that dogs help us reduce our state of arousal, which reduces blood pressure. They do that partly just by their steady presence. We can also use our dogs to fulfill a primitive and basic need, the need to touch. Touch is comforting to babies; they can be crying with distress one minute, but quiet and settled when they are held. Adults feel the same way, but often don't want to admit it. Human relationships are sometimes too complicated to let us touch and hold another person. But your dog is always available for this job.

Children with mental or physical disabilities have an especially strong bond with animals. Children who have trouble walking make astonishing efforts to maintain their balance so they can play with a dog. Those whose heads loll uncontrollably from side to side work to maintain eye contact.

Some prisons encourage inmates to keep dogs as pets, because they bring about long-term changes in attitudes and behavior. With dogs in their lives, some prisoners find out for the first time what it's like to give and receive affection.

That's the power of the human-canine bond. Although it feels unique to every person who experiences it, it's a bond that was forged many, many centuries ago.

CHAPTER 2

THE HEALING POWER OF EARLY DOGS

THE HUMAN-CANINE BOND, as we see it today, is the modern manifestation of an event that scientists say occurred more than ten thousand years ago, the domestication of the wild canine. Up until then, competition and suspicion had kept humans and canines apart. But somewhere along the line, the relationship started to change.

The traditional view has always been that human and canine forged a partnership out of necessity. Both were large mammals who hunted and ate other mammals. Canines consumed parts of the catch that man might not have wanted. It's possible that canines followed human hunters to tear apart the carcass when the human was finished with it. This would have given them positive feelings toward the human who was supplying dinner.

Some anthropologists speculate that early humans might have observed how packs of canines divided into parties, one party following the trail of the quarry, the other angling off to intercept its retreat. Early hunters may have admired this strategy and copied it, greatly increasing their chance of success. Another behavior humans may have picked up from canines is the marking of territorial boundaries, as well as marking one's trail so that it can be followed back. Dogs do this by squirting trees with urine. People refined the idea by cutting notches in trees.

At any rate, during the Neolithic period, dogs started to willingly hunt and bring back game to their human friends, despite the fact that they could have run off and consumed their own catch. Dogs decided to protect early people from dangers that threatened their survival. They turned away lions, wolves, and marauding tribes. These actions moved in the direction of the domestication of the dog, the first case of animal domestication and the only one to occur in the hunter-gatherer stage of humankind's cultural development.

Then came an event that had a profound effect on the human-canine bond; people began to live in villages.

It wasn't so much the village itself that drew the dogs. Dogs probably don't care whether humans live in caves or trees or houses. What they like is that human settlements produce a tremendous amount of waste. Early dogs hung around villages because it was a good policy. By scavenging at the village dump, they had a way to feed themselves. This led to the survival of weaker canids, ones that would not have been able to feed themselves if they had to track and kill other animals on their own. And there was a benefit for humans in this arrangement; rubbish dumps breed disease. The dog functioned as a Paleolithic garbage service.

Over the years, these canines became more and more accustomed to man, even whelping and rearing their litters within sight of human campfires. In her excellent book, *Animals in Translation*, Temple Grandin writes that sympathetic human mothers would have taken in orphaned or sick pups and cared for them. They had to do so; human biology is programmed so that oxytocin is released when we gaze at a baby or helpless creature. This natural fact of our biology led to a bond being formed between canine and human.

Dogs had another unappetizing duty. We know from anthropologists' study of Amazon and African tribes that where there were no diapers, mothers let their pet dogs be the baby wipes. It's yucky to contemplate but was marvelously effective. It was another win-win situation, too, because human feces contain a tremendous amount of protein.

In return for his aid, humans gave canines a share of their food and a corner in their dwelling. This early establishment of the human-canine bond provided humans with a wide variety of hunting, guarding, herding, transport, and companion animals to help cope with environmental and climatic change over thousands of years. The transformation of wild animals into domestic creatures that live and breed alongside humans was one of the most important events in human history.

Domestication is a tricky process. Out of the thousands of species of animals on earth, only seven became fully domesticated. Evolutionary scientists call them "The Magnificent Seven": horse, cow, sheep, goat, pig, dog, and cat. Since becoming domesticated, the dog changed from the wolf-shape into a dazzling variety of shapes and sizes, from the tiny three-pound Chihuahua to the giant 200-pound Great Dane. Until recently, no one really understood how domestication actually happened; only that it took place thousands of years ago. Our understanding of domestication was largely based on speculation.

But a forty-five-year study begun in the 1950s by the Russian geneticist Dmitry K. Belyaev of the Institute of Cytology and

Genetics in Novosibirsk, Siberia, shed amazing new light on the process. A fur-breeding farm sought Belyaev's help to create a Silver Fox that would flourish under captivity. The foxes were difficult to raise in captivity; they tended not to eat, became sick, and were too stressed to reproduce. Belyaev needed to breed a more domesticated Silver Fox. This was a good project for Belyaev since his interests lay in the domestication of animals. He believed that the key factor involved was not size or ability, but behavior—in this case, tamability. More than any other quality, Belyaev believed, tamability must have determined how well an animal would adapt to life among human beings.

In 1959, he gathered 130 wild foxes and bred together only those who showed the least fear and most acceptance of humans. In each generation, only 5 percent of the males and 20 percent of the females were kept for breeding. Students and researchers socialized the pups. From the outset, he kept records of the behavior of each generation. As expected, foxes began to behave more and more like domestic dogs. Eventually, Belyaev had foxes that would approach humans and wag their tails, a behavior not found in any wild species. (Very young wild wolf cubs wag their tails but stop when they mature.) Same with barking; now Belyaev had foxes that barked.

Belyaev was able to study 45,000 foxes. Even though he was selecting only for behavior, other, extremely surprising new aspects began to enter the gene pool. The "friendly foxes" who had never had anything but prick ears began to whelp pups with partially folded and even hanging ears, ears with soft leathers that were totally unlike those of a wild fox, but very like those of Greyhounds, Beagles, Basset Hounds, and other breeds. Wild fox ears were stiff and rigid; the "friendly fox" ears were amazingly soft and mobile.

Color began to change. The normal coat color, which had evolved as camouflage in the wild, altered, and the foxes started producing pups in a whole spectrum of colors that had never been seen before. The new foxes were sometimes white, black, brown, silver, gray, apricot, fawn, and chocolate. An even greater shock—they developed piebald coloring, one of the most striking mutations among domestic animals, but never seen in the wild. Different breeds call "piebald" by different names: particolored, broken-colored, spotted, splashed, pinto, mantle, Boston, Harlequin.

In other words, selecting for tameness and against aggression had changed the foxes biologically in ways that had nothing to do with behavior. Changes were occurring in the systems that govern the body's hormones and neurochemicals. In particular, the chemical that determined how likely the fox was to fight or flee, adrenaline, turned out to be closely linked with melanin, which determined coat color.

Additionally, after many generations, his experimental foxes began to vary greatly in size. Instead of just normal-size foxes, he now had miniature foxes, "teacup" foxes, and giant foxes.

It had always been difficult to believe that there was a single common ancestor for the great multitude of different breeds of dog, with their vast differences in size, body shape, coat, and general appearance. Belyaev's research strongly suggested that the Mastiff and Japanese Chin, the Deerhound and Pomeranian, the Saint Bernard and Bull Terrier did descend from a common progenitor.

Belyaev's research proved that domestication was not simply an adaptation in behavior. It was an adaptation to all kinds of things. The study is a landmark for evolutionists because it continued for so long. The results of his forty-five-year experiment have wide implications. It had always been thought that dogs evolved from wolves over thousands of years. Belyaev's experiment showed that it could have happened much, much quicker.

From Belyaev, we now knew more about how dogs had

evolved from wolves into canine companions for man. What we still didn't know was how those early men felt about their dogs. But that was changed by the discovery by a French archaeologist at a place in northern Israel called Ein Mallaha.

François Valla had a reputation in archaeology circles as someone who was incredibly meticulous about his dig. His group was excavating a site from the Natufian culture, carbon-dated to around 11,500 years ago, when they came across a human skeleton. Valla didn't let the excitement of the find hurry his workers. Instead of just clearing all the earth around the skeleton, he very carefully excavated the whole area. Instead of picks and shovels, he had his workers use only small brushes and dental tools.

Luckily, the site was calcareous, a condition which helps to preserve animal bone. That's how Valla came across something amazing, something never seen before at a site so ancient; evidence of affection between a human and a canine. It turned out that the skeleton was that of an old woman. She had been carefully buried in the tomb, with her dog. Her left hand was enclosed around the small dog's body.

This was the first archaeological evidence of an alliance between human and canine. It pointed to an emotional, affectionate relationship between the old woman and the dog, which scientists believe was a puppy less than six months old.

Archaeologists usually ignored animal remains at an excavation of a settlement and tended to be interested only in human skeletons. So it was possible that there had been other sites like Ein Mallaha, but in those cases canine skeletons might have been cleared away, perhaps mistaken for prehistoric rubbish.

One question that always brings up debate among dog fanciers is: Which breed of dog was the first? Saluki fanciers claim their Middle Eastern breed is oldest; Norwegian Elkhound fans claim that title for their Nordic breed. There is competition among fans of several other breeds for the title.

A geneticist from the Fred Hutchinson Cancer Research Center, Dr. Elaine Ostrander, analyzed genetic variations among eighty-five dog breeds and created a matrix by which an individual dog's breed could be identified with 99-percent accuracy. Then, by comparing dog DNA to the DNA of wolves, she determined that most of the eighty-five breeds had been created within the past two hundred years. But there was a group of fourteen breeds whose DNA showed little difference from wolves. In other words, those fourteen breeds split off from wolves very early in the evolution of the dog. This group came to be known as the "ancient breeds."

What was amazing was that the "ancient" breeds came not just from one spot, but from all over the globe. The Chow Chow, Shar-Pei, and Pekingese came from China; the Shih Tzu, Lhasa Apso, and Tibetan Terrier from Tibet; the Akita and Shiba Inu from Japan; the Afghan Hound from Afghanistan; the Saluki from the Middle East; the Basenji from central Africa; the Siberian Husky from Russia; and the Alaskan Malamute from North America. Based on DNA sampling from random spots on the canine genome, these breeds all represented close genetic matches to the wolf.

What occurred to evolutionists was that perhaps the emergence of the animal we know as the dog did not just happen once at one location. Maybe it happened *several* times in *several* places. No one region or country could claim their breed was the oldest. The creation of the dog seems to have been a simultaneous event with multiple thresholds.

For the past thousand years, dogs have been our helpers. Because they lived with us, dogs evolved new abilities to meet our needs. Doberman Pinschers guard factories. Portuguese Water Dogs pull in fishermen's nets. Sporting dogs find and retrieve game. Scent hounds find children lost in the woods or convicts escaped from prison. Dachshunds go to ground after badger. Newfoundlands rescue drowning men. Huskies and Malamutes pull sleds. Saint

Bernards dig travelers out of snow banks. Anatolian Shepherds guard the flock. Collies and Shetland Sheepdogs herd it. Greater Swiss Mountain Dogs pull a cart into town. Small dogs keep vermin out of the house and stick around to entertain.

But if we think that man's involvement with early dogs began and ended with the load he could pull and the sheep he could herd, it would be well to consider the legend of one little-known pillar of the Catholic Church, St. Roch.

CHAPTER 3

THE PATRON SAINT
OF DOGS

IN THE CENTER of Paris, close to the Champs-Élysées, the Louvre and the shopping arcades of the rue de Rivoli, there is a narrow, cool street called the rue Saint-Roch. Its gracious old buildings house quiet shops selling Chanel perfume, cabochon jewelry, and Yves Saint Laurent clothing. There are bistros and cafés where people sit quietly, glad to be out of the bustle of the big city, just a block away. There is nothing fashionable about this street, at least not in this decade. It looks like a place time forgot.

The street is narrow and short, only 1,200 feet long. Yet it contains the largest Late Baroque church in the city, the Church of Saint-Roch. It's easy to walk right past without noticing it because the street is so narrow that there is no place to stand back and fully appreciate its size. Because of its cramped location, it looks small. It's not. It is only a few feet shorter than Notre-Dame, which makes it one of the biggest in Paris. Its style is reminiscent of Saint-Sulpice, a much better known church that is also lovely, cavernous, and bathed in light reflected through beveled glass.

A statue outside the door of Saint-Roch shows a deferential but obviously holy man in monk-like robes, carrying a staff. Pressed against his side, his face turned adoringly upward, is a dog. The monk's hand rests tenderly on the dog's head. This is St. Roch.

He is not one of the Catholic Church's most popular saints. He is not St. Francis, whose image is pictured everywhere, usually with a sparrow alighting on his raised hand. He is not St. Jude, invoked constantly by the devout because he is the patron saint of lost causes. He doesn't have the cachet of St. John, with his mission to baptize all God's children, nor the steadfastness of St. Joseph. His likeness is not emblazoned on millions of medals to be worn around the neck, like St. Christopher, patron saint of travelers. A listing of popular saints would put Roch near the bottom. Yet his mission is important, exalted, and necessary.

St. Roch is the patron saint of dogs.

He was born in 1295, the son of the wealthy and noble governor of Montpellier. There was one strange thing about his birth: his chest was marked as though someone had branded him with a red cross. While he was an infant, this strange birthmark was shown widely to all the family's relatives and friends. The birthmark remained throughout his life.

Roch lived a wonderful childhood of wealth and comfort. His family was close, and its members were devoted to one another. Montpellier was an important city of the medieval period, a commercial center that had the world's finest law and medical schools.

When he was twenty, both of Roch's parents died, leaving him with riches and the governorship of a prosperous town. But instead, Roch chose the life of a pilgrim. He distributed his wealth among the poor and handed the governorship to his uncle. Roch then began his pilgrimage, setting off for Italy. According to legend, God showed his approval by giving Roch the gift of healing. At that time, the plague would appear periodically in towns and cities across Italy. When Roch stopped for a meal and a night's sleep at the Italian town of Acquapendente, he learned that the disease was decimating the townspeople.

Roch looked inward and counted himself blessed by God once again, because he was strong and healthy. As his way of giving thanks to God, Roch devoted himself to ministering to the people of Acquapendente. His prayers seemed to have special power. Many of the people he helped were cured. Roch realized that if he grew proud of this gift and sought acclaim, he would once again be far from his goal of a pious life. So he played down his healing power with the townspeople, claiming to be an ordinary ministrant and nurse. He stopped in Mantua, Modena, Parma, Rome, and other cities, finding once again other outbreaks of plague. Roch always stopped to minister to the sick.

He determined that his next stop would be the Italian town of Piacenza. Again Roch stopped and tended to the sick, and again many were cured. But in Piacenza, the most dreaded event occurred. Roch himself fell ill. When he lifted up his robes, he saw that an open sore, a sign of the plague, had invaded his leg just above the knee.

Roch felt that perhaps this was his call from God to join him in the afterlife. The gift of healing had flowed through him for several years, but now his own time had finally come. According to some accounts, he didn't want the villagers to see his suffering, as he knew they would tend to him and possibly reinfect themselves and others. Roch disappeared and went to a quiet spot in the woods to live out his days. He made a hut of boughs and leaves, which was miraculously supplied with water from a spring that arose nearby.

A dog followed him to his hiding place, which may not have

seemed unusual in a land where dogs roamed free. The next day, the same dog appeared, this time carrying a loaf of bread. Roch tried to shoo him away, but the dog wouldn't go. Again and again, the dog returned to Roch's side, offering the bread. Finally it occurred to Roch that the dog was on a mission of his own. He wanted Roch to eat the bread. It filled his empty stomach, and this made the dog happy. When Roch finally fell asleep, the dog was still there, warming him with his own body and gently licking the plague sores on his legs.

The next day, the dog appeared again, with another loaf. And every day thereafter. With this dog as his source of sustenance, Roch was slowly regaining his strength.

The appearance of the dog with the bread was a miracle to Roch. But at the same time, bread was disappearing from the table of the nobleman who owned the woods, Lord Gothard. He noticed that his dog did not devour the bread, but carried it away to the forest. One day, he followed his dog to see where he was taking the bread. The dog led him to Roch.

Lord Gothard thought at first that a beggar or tramp had won his dog's favor. He thought he would find some kind of poacher or hunter hiding in his woods. He was not prepared for the sight of a pious and humble holy man.

Lord Gothard wanted to take Roch into his home, but Roch refused. So the nobleman ministered to Roch himself, as Roch had ministered to so many others. God worked his miracle and Roch was able to recover. When he was strong enough, he agreed to visit Lord Gothard's castle, where Roch found friendship and the means to start over in life as a healer.

Restored to health, Roch was called on to minister to the cardinal of Angleria in Lombardy, who had fallen ill. Through prayer and by making the mark of the cross on his forehead, Roch healed him. Even when the cardinal was well again, the cross on his forehead miraculously remained.

Finally Roch decided to return to Montpellier. His uncle was not pleased to hear that his nephew was on his way. Roch was taken prisoner outside town on suspicion of being a spy, and he refused to say who he was. This time, there was no small dog to help him. He was imprisoned, and after five years of confinement, he died in 1327. When his body was prepared for burial, there happened to be guards present who had worked many years for his family. They were astonished to see the unmistakable birthmark, the red cross, on Roch's chest and told others, who were equally devastated to learn of Roch's imprisonment and death. He was given a grand funeral in the cathedral. People began to pray to him and made statues in his likeness, placing them in the area's churches and chapels, always with a dog by his side.

Those who knew of his healing work in Italy venerated him. In Montpellier, a chapel and a feast day was dedicated to him in the early 1400s, by which time he was popularly considered a saint, the one to pray to in order to keep safe from pestilence. Around that time another infestation of plague, the Black Death, spread through Europe. Devout Catholics believed that it was their prayers to St. Roch that brought an end to it. He was officially canonized in 1629, some two hundred years after his death.

The citizens of Paris started building the church of Saint-Roch around 1650. Louis XIV laid the cornerstone. As was the norm during that period, money was short, and the construction period was long. The church was finally finished in 1740. Many famous people are buried in this medieval church, among them, the playwright Pierre Corneille, the royal gardener André LeNôtre and the philosopher Denis Diderot. It is a treasure house of religious painting and sculpture by such artists as J. B. Pierre, Michel Anguier, François Le Moyne, and Étienne Maurice Falconet, much of it from now-vanished churches and monasteries.

The day I visited, I sought out the sacristan with a question of personal interest that had been bothering me ever since I learned of St. Roch: What *breed* of dog saved St. Roch from the plague? In Italian paintings, he is often shown as a small Whippet. Outside this Paris church, the saint was caressing a French Shepherd. Was there any ruling on what breed the dog actually was? The priest listened politely to my question, *Était-ce un berger ou un levrier?* Was he a shepherd or a sighthound?

He gave an impatient shrug and told me to go look at the paintings. It seems odd that in a culture that traditionally loves its dogs and takes them everywhere with them, they pay so little attention to the dog's patron saint.

St. Roch is more recognized in his role as patron saint of people who are victims of mass illness than as the patron saint of dogs. Maybe devout dog owners haven't prayed to him quite enough.

There is one place in France, however, where St. Roch's special connection with dogs is happily celebrated every year: in the ancient city of Toulouse in the southwest. Frère Pelegrin, whose usual job is to show English-speaking tourists the modest quarters of Dominic, another Catholic saint, is lavish in his enthusiasm for the parade held to mark St. Roch's birthday. In broken English and with sweeping arm gestures, he described how, on the second Sunday of August, the population gathers up all their pet dogs and walks them happily through the streets behind a procession of priests, novitiates, nuns, and various devout and non-devout Catholics. The procession ends at the cathedral, where a Mass is said in honor of dogs, and the priest joyously blesses them. Altar boys enthusiastically sprinkle the dogs with holy water so they can carry the blessing home. He said that a similar festival is held at the Chapel San Rocco in Venice, but that the French festival is better because, after all, Roch was born in Southern France.

Throughout the southern French region of Languedoc, nearly every chapel along the pilgrimage route called the Compostela de Santiago contains a statue of St. Roch. The loyal dog is always by his side. Often, the dog is sculpted licking the plague sore, symbolic of the healing act of dog given to man.

The cult of St. Roch came to America, specifically to New Orleans, with a German priest, Father Peter Leonard Thevis. In 1868, New Orleans was struck by an epidemic of yellow fever. Father Thevis knew the story of St. Roch, known also by his Italian name, St. Rocco, and urged the parishioners of Holy Trinity Church to pray to him.

As yellow fever blanketed the city and more and more people died, Father Thevis implored St. Roch in his prayers to keep his parishioners well. If they survived the fever, he promised he would build a chapel to St. Roch with his own hands.

Not a single parishioner of Holy Trinity died.

Father Thevis kept his word. The Gothic-style chapel and cemetery that he built were completed in 1876. On the altar is a statue of St. Roch and his faithful dog. Many people take their prayers to St. Roch there. On the walls are many artificial limbs and crutches, left behind by grateful supplicants whose prayers were answered.

When you see a statue or portrait of St. Roch, the faithful dog is usually sitting by his side. Earlier painters often portrayed the dog licking his wound, which might sound disgusting until you learn that medical researchers have found there is a small amount of antibiotic in a dog's saliva. It's nothing compared to the strength of the drugs we have today, but maybe several hundred years ago, it did make a difference.

People believed from early times that the dog's power to heal was physical. Some of the strongest proponents of that belief were not in St. Roch's environs at all, but half a planet away, on the North American continent. They were the people of a great civilization who became known as the Aztecs.

CHAPTER 4

THE WARM TOUCH OF THE ZOLO

THE AZTECS WERE the dominant nation in Mexico before the Spanish conquest in the sixteenth century. They were a people rich in history, art, science, religion, and gold, and they extended their rule over a large portion of Mesoamerica and the other peoples who lived there. But the conquistadors usurped the Aztecs' empire and stole their sculptures, gems, and gold.

The conquistadors didn't fully understand Aztec culture, partly because their religion included human sacrifice and, occasionally, cannibalism. That came to an end with the Spanish conquest and the massive epidemics that devastated the Indian population soon after the Spaniards' arrival. Nevertheless, the Aztecs were a highly developed people: they built vast cities and monumental architecture; developed an almost impossibly intricate and accurate calendar; were the first in the world to make education compulsory for all citizens, regardless of gender or social rank; laid the basis for Mexican cuisine; and bred dogs who, they believed, possessed mystical powers.

Clay figures and remains of Xolos, dating back from 300 to 900 A.D., have been found in burial sites. Aztec high priests believed that when a human died, a dog would lead the soul of its dead owner through the underworld. A dog was sacrificed at every burial for this purpose. They also thought their dogs were spirits sent by the god Xolotl (the god of fire, lightning, and death) to guide them in life. One unique aspect of these Aztec dogs, a breed known today as the Xolo, was their hairlessness. Unlike the Chihuahua, a Toltec Indian breed from as early as the ninth century A.D. (descendant of the "Techichi" dog), most of the Aztecs' Xolo dogs had no coat at all, just soft skin. The body temperature of a Xolo is the same as any other dog, but because they are hairless, one is able to feel the warmth of their bodies directly. So the Aztecs placed them in their beds to be used like heating pads. They then discovered that the warmth the hairless dogs generated had the "magical" power to stop or alleviate pain in joints, stomachs, and so forth. So they draped Xolos over their necks, knees, and hips. The full named of the breed is *Xoloitzcuintli*, which is derived from combining the name of the Aztec Indian god Xolotl and the Aztec word for dog, *itzcuintli*. Today the Xolo breed is more commonly known as the Mexican Hairless.

Nancy Gordon had no idea of the historical therapeutic aspect of Xolos when she first met one such dog in 1999. She was simply visiting a friend who was delighted with her new Xolo puppy. Nancy admits that she was no dog lover at the time. She had never owned a dog.and dogs were never a part of her family's traditions. She certainly didn't covet her friend's new pup. She was simply petting him on her lap when she noticed how warm he was. She surreptitiously stuck her aching wrist under him. Fifteen minutes later, the pain disappeared.

Nancy was shocked. She saw immediately that the potential use of this dog was enormous. She was living on disability because of chronic fatigue immunodeficiency syndrome and fibromyalgia syndrome, a form of chronic pain she suffered from after a serious car crash. She was constantly searching for relief. She went to specialists, well-known clinics, and chronic pain centers. She tried every new medication that came on the market. She took herbs and adjusted her diet. She tried physical therapy, massage, exercise, crystals, energy healers, and hypnosis. She did a great deal of research. She was willing to try anything. But nothing helped for more than a few minutes.

She found that the best tool in her arsenal to fight pain was a heating pad. Heat relieved her symptoms for brief periods of time; she always kept microwavable heating pads nearby. Yet her condition grew worse, to the point that she could no longer do her job as a licensed clinical social worker. She closed her private practice and moved from Oregon to San Diego in order to live near family members and under a warm sun.

After the surprising meeting with the Xolo, she began an immediate search for one of her own. She discovered that breeders and fanciers prefer the original name for the breed, Xoloitzcuintli, or Xolos, rather than Mexican Hairless. When Nancy eventually found the right puppy, she named her Toaster.

Nancy had achieved a great deal in her life. Before her injury, she was in constant motion, always bouncing into new situations with her auburn curls and bright teal eyes. It had sometimes seemed as if her high energy could barely fit into her small frame. But she had never trained a dog, so she worried about how to go about it.

Toaster solved that problem for her right away. From the beginning, Toaster would willingly wrap her warm little body around Nancy's aching neck. She pressed herself up against her back. She seemed happy to provide this service. "She sometimes scrambles so fast to get up to my neck that she slips. She does this job as if it were something she was born to do."

Doctors have long known that heat provides relief from pain by increasing blood circulation and allowing tissues to stretch. That means less stiffness and greater flexibility. The usual heat therapies are hot baths, showers, hot packs, a heating pad, or a heat lamp. No one had ever prescribed hot dogs.

Besides their body temperature, there are other ways that Xolos may help humans, and that is the healing power of touch. Science has shown that physical contact against a patient's skin can block transmission of pain from the central nervous system. Xolos are all about touch. They love to hug and cuddle, placing their soft skin against yours.

Beyond that, there are the reasons why dogs in general may help patients. Studies show that most people relax when they are around dogs. The relaxation response loosens muscles and tends to ease pain. Also, people tend to cheer up around dogs. And when people talk to a dog, the pain of silence is relieved. When you walk a dog, you exercise, which is sometimes the best medicine. Putting it simply, dogs help people get out of a state of depression.

Toaster and Nancy became inseparable. Nancy could work longer at her computer with Toaster warming her neck. She could drive longer distances with Toaster snuggled down against her lower back. And she no longer felt isolated and alone with her illness, because Toaster was with her. Almost everything in her life became better because of Toaster.

Never mind that the breed is generally the hands-down winner in "Ugly Dog of the Year" contests. Not many people are attracted to the breed's hairless, tough skin in black, gray, red, liver, or bronze. For most people, appreciation of the Xolo is a matter of taste or acclimation. For Nancy, it was love at first sight. In her eyes, they are the most beautiful breed in the world.

Nancy enrolled in a program called "Leashes for Living" in San Diego to train Toaster as a service dog. That way, they could always legally be together, even in markets, movie theaters, or at restaurants. Toaster could also accompany Nancy on a plane and not have to ride in a carrier.

The training was grueling; she and Toaster went three times a month for eight hours a day, in a class with seven other students. It took three years of training to make it to graduation. Now Toaster proudly wore the yellow-and-blue "service dog" vest. She had learned how to pick up things Nancy dropped, open and close cupboards and doors, and bring her bottle of pills from her purse. Nancy says with a smile: "Sometimes it's not the first thing she brings. But she always goes back and tries again."

Even though Toaster's mouth is tiny with few teeth—toothlessness is genetically related to hairlessness—she can pull off socks and tug on sleeves. She can pick up a coin or a credit card off the floor.

In all, Toaster knows around 120 words and commands. For Nancy's specific condition, Toaster has been trained to lie across her neck when she asks, "Neck, please."

"Toaster has helped me in so many ways," Nancy says. "One of the things I taught her was to sing with me when I am having a bad day. She even has her own theme song, 'Tostada,' sung to the tune of 'Volare.'"

Nancy finds that Toaster is so incredibly intelligent and intuitive that she anticipates what Nancy needs. For instance, Nancy must rest often to keep up her strength and not let her pain wear her down. That means she can only work at her computer for short periods of time. But she recalled a day, early in Toaster's training, when she was researching Xolos on the Internet. Nancy was excited by the sites she found and wanted to read each one, so she stayed in her chair, despite the aching pain that kept increasing.

Toaster came to her side, trying to attract her attention. "What is it?" she asked hurriedly. She got up and went to the door to see if Toaster needed to go out. No, that wasn't it. She went into the kitchen and checked her water bowl. It was full. So that wasn't it, either. She gave up guessing and went back to the Internet. Fifteen minutes later, Toaster was at her side again, pawing and rubbing. Nancy looked at her. What could she possibly want? She and Toaster had just begun to learn a new command at school. Nancy decided to try that and said, "Show me." Toaster walked out of the room, craning her neck to make sure Nancy was following. They passed the kitchen and went down the hall. Toaster turned into Nancy's bedroom and leapt onto the bed, giving Nancy a look as if to say, "This is what I'm trying to tell you."

A light bulb went on in Nancy's brain; Toaster was trying to tell her to lie down because she was in pain! Although Nancy hadn't asked Toaster to help her, Toaster knew that it was time to do just that.

Nancy was amazed that Toaster had been able to communicate with her so effectively. "The more you pay attention to communicating with your dog, the more you realize how much they can communicate. She had something to tell me, and she wouldn't give up until I understood."

Toaster is a Coated Xolo (as opposed to the Hairless). Her body is covered with very short fur, like that of a Miniature Pinscher or Manchester Terrier. But the fur is so thin that even coated Xolos give off enough warmth to be pain relievers. Mated to a hairless Xolo, Toaster had a litter of four puppies, two hairless and two coated. Nancy placed three of the puppies with people suffering from chronic pain. She kept Pink, a hairless female, who completed service-dog training and now shares duties with Toaster.

"Pink must be half-retriever. She loves to retrieve. She knows fourteen items by name, including the names of four different remote-control units of the entertainment system. She knows the difference between the cell phone and cordless phone."

When Pink hears Nancy's cellphone ring, she hunts it down and retrieves it quickly enough for Nancy to take the call, without being asked. Pink won First Prize in a Best Trick contest for performing that feat. Nancy says: "Pink loves to be of service. She is so happy to get you anything you want. When she can't figure out what you want, watching her mind work is amazing.

"Once, an important document blew out of my hands and went down the street. I was desperate to get it back but it moved out of reach again. Pink ran over to it, but dogs can't pick paper off the ground. There's nothing to hold onto. She tried several different times, but couldn't get it. Finally, she licked the paper so it came up enough so she could grab it with her teeth. She brought it back without a mark on it."

The story of Toaster and her puppies was filmed by Animal Planet and made into a segment for their series, That's My Baby! Every time the segment airs, Nancy is deluged with calls from pain sufferers wanting to know where they can get a Xolo. There aren't many breeders, because it's a rare breed.

The colonial-era Spanish are partly responsible for making them so rare. As they didn't know about the Xoloitzcuintli's healing power, the dogs may have seemed like useless mouths to feed. They couldn't guard homes or pull carts or herd sheep or retrieve ducks. In fact, there was only one use the Spanish could think of for the Xolos: They found them delicious. The writer Francisco Javier Clavijero wrote in 1778 that Spaniards killed thousands of them and salted the meat for their long voyages back to Spain.

The breed survived in small numbers over the centuries. As the Aztecs were assimilated into the general mestizo population of Mexico, a few Xolos remained with them. Luckily, some families still prized the breed for their healing power on rheumatic joints and sore muscles, and it became established again in central

Mexico. In the early 1900s, American diplomats living in Mexico City brought Xolos back to the United States. Because of their carefully documented Mexican pedigrees and obvious breed type, the American Kennel Club accepted Xoloitzcuintlis as a registerable breed.

But by 1950, a decade had passed in which none were registered. The AKC figured the breed was extinct and removed Xoloitzcuintle from the list.

Recent decades have seen a rising interest in all sorts of rare breeds. People who wanted an exotic pet started to discover Xolos, breed them, exhibit them, and form fan clubs. The breed has enough supporters that the AKC reinstated it into their registry in 1997.

Other breeds of hairless dogs exist—the Chinese Crested, the Peruvian Hairless, the Peruvian Inca Orchid, and the American Hairless Terrier—but it's best not to ask Nancy Gordon about those. She will tactfully reply that she's never owned one, so she can't say what they are like to live with. She's seen them at Pet Expos, and "their temperaments are different," she says. "For Xolos, this is their history. This is what they have done for thousands of years."

Even in her roles as friend, heating pad, and smartest, cleverest, most loving, versatile dog that every lived, Toaster wasn't finished with Nancy yet. There was yet another role the dog was to play.

One of the most devastating effects of Nancy's illness was the loss of her career. She had worked hard to help others as a clinical social worker. After her car crash, pain, exhaustion, and memory loss forced her to stop working. The lack of fulfilling work was a huge hole in her life.

"One day, I glanced over at Toaster, and she was holding this cup in her mouth. She looked so funny it made me laugh. I thought, 'I've got to take a photo,' but I had to walk in front of Toaster into the kitchen, pick up my camera and come back, focus, and then take the shot. While I did all of that, Toaster kept absolutely still. It was strange behavior for her. Usually she would drop the cup and start doing something else. But this time, she made sure that I got a perfect shot."

When the photos were developed, Nancy looked at Toaster's pose and thought, "greeting card." An idea hit her: She could make greeting cards. Beginning with this initial shot of Toaster, she brought out a special and successful line of cards for people who have chronic or terminal illnesses. "They are cards for when 'Get Well Soon' is just not appropriate," Nancy says. "They are for patients who are never going to get completely well. They are just hoping for some pain-free days."

The National Fibromyalgia Association ran an article about Toaster in its magazine, which resulted in another deluge of requests for puppies from her. Nancy tries to speak with each person and shares her experiences.

The number of people suffering from fibromyalgia syndrome and chronic fatigue immunodeficiency syndrome form a large and growing part of the population. For those disabled by those conditions, there is no designated type of service dog. Clearly, Xolos could fill that role.

Nancy has decided to form a nonprofit agency to attract funding so that she can breed Xolos and place them with people suffering from chronic pain. She says that as far as she knows she is the first person to try to build an organization encouraging the use of Xolos as service dogs. She named her mission "X-CPR," or "Xolos for Chronic Pain Relief."

⌒

PINK NOW HAS a disability of her own. She was born with a defective knee cap. She was operated on when she was one-year-old, and the veterinarian discovered to her horror that there was more trouble than just the patella. The bones had fused improperly and were causing her tremendous pain every day of her life. The vet asked for Nancy's permission to remove her leg. Nancy says: "Up to that point in my life, the hardest decision I had ever made was to close my practice. This was the second hardest. I agonized over it because I didn't know if Pink would be able to go on living her life the way she wanted, very active and constantly retrieving things."

Because Pink's health was in jeopardy, Nancy had to agree. She was waiting anxiously in a treatment room a few days after the surgery, eager to take Pink home. "If I could describe how she looked that day, when she realized her leg was gone—she was mad. It gives me chills to remember how angry she looked. If you can say a dog was livid, she was livid. Poor thing. I felt so sorry for her.

"But she's shown me you don't give up. You get over the handicap and keep on going. Now, she retrieves as well as she ever did. She lives to retrieve. Dogs live so much in the moment. They don't hold grudges. If they get burned on the stove, they learn not to touch the stove again, but they don't get mad at the stove."

Toaster's other puppies also work as service dogs for ailing people in Denver and California. Nancy was able to obtain two Xolos from Mexico and placed those. Then there was a man who owned a pair, but who had a terminal illness. He wanted his beloved dogs to be placed as service dogs for others.

"I can't imagine my life without my dogs now," Nancy says. "Toaster changed my life. She saved my soul. She gave me another opportunity to find a mission in life. She is the inspiration for using my experience to help other people. The nurturing side of me that was a therapist—I thought I'd lost that. Toaster gave that opportunity back to me."

As Nancy settles back into the sofa, Toaster wraps herself behind Nancy's bouncy red curls. Pink leaps up on her lap, gives Nancy a kiss, and settles down to warm her stomach.

The amazing ability of Toaster and Pink to heal Nancy Gordon physically is greatly enhanced by their ability to intuit what she needs. She is wrapped in the healing power of their warm bodies and also in the great love they bear for her. That love is at the center of all human-canine bonds. Nancy was purposefully seeking such a relationship when she acquired Toaster. But it sometimes comes even to people who are not seeking it, people like Russie McDerment-Fogarty. She was just looking for a nice pet to add to her household. But she got much more than that in Kyle.

CHAPTER 5

THE HEALING POWER OF KYLE

THE FIRST THING THAT Russie McDerment-Fogarty will tell you about her Scottish Terrier, Kyle, is that he was an angel who appointed himself her guardian and stayed close by her side for many years. He was one of six Scottish Terriers she has owned in her life, and while she loved all of them, Kyle was special.

"In all my years of owning and dearly loving Scotties, I have to say that he alone has left the biggest mark in our lives. There was just something truly unique and almost magical about him."

What makes Russie shake her head in wonderment is that she didn't even want Kyle. When she was first making inquiries about acquiring a dog, she spoke with a Florida breeder who told her about Morgan, a three-year-old champion bitch who had raised two litters of puppies.

Both of Morgan's parents were well-known show dogs.

Her brother was a successful Scottish Terrier sire. All this meant that the breeder's dogs had in spades all the distinct breed characteristics that Russie loved: the perky upright ears, long clean skull, black beard, cobby body, short legs, and twinkling eyes. And the breeder was looking for a retirement home where she'd be loved and appreciated. Russie persuaded her husband to make a whirlwind drive from their small town in West Virginia to Florida to pick up Morgan.

The moment she saw Morgan, she loved her. Russie ignored a six-month-old male puppy bumbling around the house. She didn't like his brindle coat, a sort of gray, grizzled with black. And this puppy had a major fault: achondroplasia, a shortening of the cartilage and bones, which gave him strangely bowed legs. And he had another obvious fault: his mouth was undershot.

But the breeder told her: "I don't think Morgan should be alone. You need another Scottie."

Russie looked at the little dog that most Scottie lovers would find unattractive. The breeder encouraged, "He's one of the smartest Scotties I've ever owned." Kyle turned his head and directed his small, bright eyes at her. What caught her attention was something about his expression, not just some eager and "varminty" quality, as the American Kennel Club standard called it, but the wise look of an elder human. So, after a quick consultation with her husband, she agreed to take Kyle home.

The joy of having two beautiful Scotties in her life gave Russie a boost. It was fun to come home from work every day with those two little creatures to greet her. Kyle's strange physical faults amused Russie. His bowed legs made him bounce when he walked. His underbite made his little tongue poke out, which looked cute and pink when he slept.

One morning, Russie was struck by a migraine headache as she was getting ready for work. She had been plagued since childhood by migraines. She had once heard a reference to a "minor" migraine, wishing someday to know what that would be like. For her, and for the other female members of her family, migraines were a horrible curse that arrived like a strong slap and stayed for several hours or several days. Nauseated and unsteady, she felt the throbbing, pounding, pulsating pain in her head, worse on the right side than the left. Unable to stand any light, she pulled shut the curtains and turned off the lamp. Then there was the exhaustion; fatigue so great she felt it was too much work to lift even her hand to pat the little Scottie head that appeared in front of her.

Morgan sensed Russie's distress and quietly kept her distance. Kyle sensed it and moved closer to her, sitting next to her on Russie's husband's pillow, studying her seriously. Usually nothing could get through the pain of the migraine, but this morning Russie was aware that Kyle was there and that he wanted to help. There was nothing to be done. She just had to wait it out. But this time, at least, she was not alone.

Kyle was a dog who liked to play with his toys. He liked to go for walks and keep watch on what was going on outside the house, in case any insolent squirrels decided to hang around or rabbits dashed too close. Those things were important to him. But when Russie was sick, he abandoned his usual routine and stayed by her side. Not just her side; he sensed where the source of pain was, and wanted to be close to her head, to where she literally hurt. The migraines were so bad she was sometimes in bed for two or three days. Kyle was there every minute. The bow-legged puppy she hadn't wanted grew into the most devoted dog she had ever owned.

He appeared to know exactly the right thing to do at the right moment. Russie calls him "soulful." When she got a migraine, everything in his life would stop until she got better. She searched out a specialist in Washington, D.C., who had new medicines and procedures. The migraines grew further apart and were less painful. Russie was grateful to Kyle, because she felt it was in some way his concern that had given her the determination to find better treatment.

A few years later, a veterinary specialist discovered that Morgan had mammary cancer. She underwent surgery immediately in order to have a chain of affected glands removed. She seemed to recover fully.

But a year later Russie began to suspect that, once again, something was wrong with Morgan. She couldn't put her finger on it, but Morgan just seemed a little quiet, a little off. "I took her over to Virginia Tech and wanted them to ultrasound her. They wouldn't do it because they said there was no reason. They couldn't find anything wrong with her. But I know my dogs. I knew something wasn't right."

The results of a recheck by a surgeon revealed that Morgan turned out to have a highly progressed transitional cell bladder cancer. "They said, 'You'll get four months with her if you're lucky.'" Russie was determined to be lucky. She devoted herself to caring for Morgan. After Morgan had outlived the prognosis by a year, she received chemotherapy that was suggested by the vets. But the dosage of chemo drugs she received proved to be too intense for her body, and she had to be hospitalized.

When Russie came home without her, Kyle was confused. For a while, he sat alone in corners. But, maybe because dogs are social animals, he discovered a way to have contact with humans that didn't involve Russie. He started watching TV.

Kyle was seven years old. He'd never shown an interest in TV before. He usually slept in bed with Russie, while Morgan took the dog bed alongside. Now, instead of sleeping, Kyle went to the foot of the bed and sat down, intently watching the television screen. When Russie and her husband fell asleep, he was still watching, so they often left it on for him. "When I got up to go to work in the morning, he'd be watching it. I'd leave it on for him all day. I hated to turn it off because it was so important to him.

"He seemed to become more and more aware of what was going on in the programs. My husband was into watching *The Sopranos*. Kyle watched with him, but he would get really upset when people got killed. Or even if there was something harsh, like hitting another guy with a baseball bat or driving into someone with a car. He hated PBS, documentaries, or anything educational like that, the kind of things I like to watch. He would give me a look like, 'Change the channel!'"

In a slightly embarrassed voice, Russie admits, "If there was a program I really wanted to watch, I had to go watch it in another room."

Kyle also liked news programs, but Russie noticed that he seemed to hate one particular person who was appearing on the screen a lot that winter. It was Scott Petersen, the husband who was eventually found guilty of killing his wife, Laci. "From the first time he ever saw him on television, he would bark and go crazy and try to bite the screen. And this was just during the time that Laci had disappeared, and they had no idea who did it. Kyle knew!"

Morgan finally came home from the hospital. But she wasn't doing well. Russie often had to get up in the middle of the night to carry her out, because she had cerebellar ataxia, a disorder of the nervous system that affects balance and coordination and made her walking unstable, almost like a drunken sailor. Kyle continued his TV watching, as if he could not bear to see his friend so ill. "I don't mean watching in a small way, I mean literally addicted to TV. At first it was funny, but later, it was worrisome. My veterinarian just laughed when I told him about it. He said it would probably pass. Occasionally, Kyle would growl at the bad guys or at cats and dogs, but mostly he just watched in silence."

During her visit to the vet for her last chemotherapy session, harmful bacteria and their toxins took hold in her tissues. Morgan wasn't strong enough to overcome this setback. She died in the hospital.

Russie was devastated. Even though Morgan had been sick for a long time, at the end, death was sudden. A veterinarian who was studying cerebellar abiotrophy pleaded with Russie to have Morgan's brain necropsied. Russie realized the research was important, so she agreed. She left Morgan's body at the vet for a week for the procedure. When her husband went to pick up the body for burial, it had been in a freezer.

Russie laid her frozen body on the floor and opened the plastic bag. "I was so relieved to see that she still looked beautiful—like nothing had happened." Russie brought Kyle over to the body. She felt he needed to see that Morgan was dead so he would stop waiting for her to come home.

When Kyle realized this inert body was Morgan, he went and picked up the only toy Morgan liked, a brightly colored birthday hat from Petsmart. He put it beside her and tottered back and forth on his feet, something he did when he was anxious. But instead of gaining the closure that Russie hoped for, Kyle seemed angry. He seemed to blame her for Morgan's death. And he kept staring suspiciously at Russie's husband, Patrick.

After that day, Kyle would not sleep on Russie's bed. "I tried to take walks with him and do special things with him alone, but nothing made any difference."

As a final insult, Kyle got up on their bed and peed on Pat's side.

Kyle still distracted himself from his grief by watching TV. But now, he wouldn't watch in the same room where Russie and Pat were. He would go sit in another room and wait for them to turn on the TV there. He didn't want anything to do with his owners.

Next, they took Kyle for a beach vacation to the Outer Banks of North Carolina. Even in this secluded spot, he still kept his distance. Russie missed his presence at her side. And Russie grew even more depressed at the situation.

Russie couldn't take it anymore. So on the third night of vacation, she scooped up Kyle and took him down to the beach with her. Under a full Carolina moon, with a thunderstorm approaching and the ocean lapping at their feet, she told Kyle how much she missed him. His reaction was to move farther away. But she pressed him against her. She started to talk, telling him the story of Morgan's cerebellar abiotrophy and why the necropsy was necessary.

"In short, I explained everything that had happened in the last months, and said anything that might reassure him. I swear he listened to me, because the trip back to the house was so different; he practically skipped back. He seemingly came back to our beach house a different dog. Most significantly, he slept with us again that night. And he resumed giving me kisses."

Five years later, it was Kyle's turn to be sick. He was genetically challenged, as Morgan had been. He had irritable bowel syndrome, food allergies, and liver disease. He had to have teeth pulled because they'd been forced out of alignment by his underbite. He had to have biopsies done on his feet. The veterinarian took an eye-shaped piece of skin from each of his front pads and removed skin tags from several places on his body. It was painful; he grumbled at Russie to tell her so. Kyle was so upset that he boycotted Russie for three days. She got down on the floor with him and showed him the scars from her appendectomy and gallbladder operations. She had a scar on her wrist from a malunion that was re-set. She told him she'd put him through this only in order to make sure he was going to be okay.

With all his other medical problems under control, Kyle developed the one Russie had been dreading: bladder cancer. (Unfortunately, it is a common cancer in Scotties. They are eighteen times more likely to get it than any other breed.) Morgan had lived for more than two years with bladder cancer. Russie hoped Kyle would manage even longer because they'd caught it so early. She devoted herself to his treatment.

Then Russie noticed strange behavior from Kyle. He was giving her extremely vigorous kisses on the face, targeting a particular spot on her cheek. At first, she had no idea why. But a few weeks after he started, she noticed a sore spot in her mouth that wouldn't heal. She asked her dentist about it, who sent her to an oral surgeon. The surgeon did a biopsy and said it was okay. But Kyle still would not stop kissing that spot.

Meanwhile, Kyle wasn't doing well. In March, Russie took him to Purdue University to undergo photodynamic therapy for his bladder cancer. When Russie brought him home from this ordeal, he was frantic to get next to her so he could keep kissing that one spot on her face.

Her surgeon had told her there was nothing wrong. So what did Kyle find so compelling about this one spot on her face? Russie didn't want to act like a hypochondriac. After all, wouldn't it be crazy to call the doctor and say, "My dog thinks there's something wrong with my face." But Kyle was insistent. To ease her mind, Russie went back to the dentist and asked him to recheck the sore spot. She underwent another biopsy. The results were grave. She had Stage Two oral squamous cell carcinoma.

Her condition was so serious that the surgeons had to remove one-third of her tongue and part of the floor of her mouth. Not satisfied that they had caught all the cancer, they did a modified radical neck dissection to search for cancerous lymph nodes. This meant more weeks in the hospital. Her husband kept her updated with twice daily phone calls. He told her the truth: Kyle was failing. "As scared as I was about my own situation, I was completely preoccupied with what would happen to him." By insisting there was something wrong with her face, he had probably saved her life. If he died suddenly, the way Morgan had, she wouldn't even get to say good-bye.

When the hospital chaplain came to pray with her, Russie began to sob. She asked if he would mind if they talked about her dog. She worried he'd disapprove, because after all, his work was saving people's souls. But without missing a beat, he leaned in to listen. She told him how Kyle's insistence led her to get a second opinion. If she'd waited any longer, who knew what might have happened? The chaplain showed no urge to chastise her when she said that Kyle was a strong inspiration to her to get better.

Russie finally came home, tired and in a great deal of pain. Kyle was overjoyed to see her. He sniffed her cheek, but instead of kissing it insistently, the way he had before, his kisses were gentle. Just having Kyle was better medicine than pills.

Oral cancer causes 8,000 deaths a year; one person dies of it every hour of every day. The statistics on oral cancer recurrences are extremely high. Patients who survive a first encounter with it have a twenty times higher risk of developing it a second time. The heightened risk factors last for five to ten years.

Russie was scared. Her Christian faith and being home with her husband and Kyle were the two things that gave her hope. Together, these made her want to believe not in statistics, but in getting well.

As her strength started to return, she noticed Kyle was weakening. His bladder cancer was getting worse. "They suggested we take him in for this new treatment. They insert a special dye in the bladder, and then put an ultraviolet light through this really small catheter and the dye reacts with the light. And the cancer cells die and slough off. Kyle had an allergic reaction to the dye. They don't know what happened. They had to keep him for four extra days. After that he went downhill. I was distraught because not only had we spent four thousand dollars doing this to him, at the end, it had made him worse."

His liver disease—a problem for most of his life—also gained ground. He ended up in the veterinary hospital for a severe bout of pancreatitis. Every day of that week, Russie sat by his cage in the hospital, encouraging him to get better. Whenever he lifted his head, he saw her there.

He eventually came home, but as the weeks passed, he grew steadily weaker. Now it was his bladder cancer that was accelerating. Russie cooked his food and supplemented his diet with special herbs, but he seemed to feel worse all the time. They watched television together, seriously considering the Weather Channel, *The Today Show*, *American Idol*, *CSI*, Animal Planet, National Geographic, and *Curb Your Enthusiasm*.

"When it was time for Kyle to go, he let me know in his typically intelligent fashion. He stopped eating and drinking for several days. His message was loud and clear. On the third day, I woke up and saw him looking at me in discomfort. I asked him plainly what he wanted. That's when he just blinked. He 'told' me he was done. There was no mistake about what he wanted. Kyle had a difficult day, shivering and whining in pain until the vet could get to us.

"My mother came to be with Kyle—just like she would have attended the death of anyone in her family. We all sat around him on the floor, weeping. When the vet got there, I gathered Kyle up on my lap and nuzzled his ears and smelled his sweet scent for the last time.

"He lived just long enough to see me healed and healthy, and then he went on his way. I ask God to keep him safe for me until we can be reunited once more. I look forward to that day because I know Kyle is waiting for me."

Kyle died in August, leaving Russie feeling depressed and depleted. She was still in mourning on her birthday, November 3, when the phone rang and a friend asked for a favor. Her brother's little boy had suffered a brain injury, and the family was spending all their time at the hospital. They had a Scottish Terrier, who was now spending long days sitting in her crate. Would Russie mind taking care of her?

"They brought her over at midnight. When I saw her, I couldn't believe it. I picked her up and looked at her. She had this funny twinkle in her eye, as if she and I shared a secret. And she looked a little like Kyle. She and I connected from the moment we met."

When Russie spoke, the terrier, Amy, would sit and listen attentively, just as Kyle had. She liked the same video and game sites on the Internet that Kyle enjoyed, like Prannoch.com. When Russie switched on the television, instead of curling up on a dog bed, Amy sat down next to her and focused on the screen. She was watching TV, just as Kyle had.

"I know the Lord sent her to me, but I felt like Kyle had a hand in it. And it was my *birthday*. The way she just appeared, out of the blue, on that exact day...." Russie shakes her head in wonder. "She's not Kyle, but she's special."

Russie has a checkup every month. It's been a year, and there are no new skin lesions.

"He enriched my life like no other pet. I was blessed by this little dog. I still hear him barking in the night, asking me to get up and let him out. I'll wake up and wonder if his spirit is still in this room. He will never be truly gone from this house, so long as I live. And he will live on in my heart for a lifetime."

One of the things that makes Russie's story so compelling is the wonderful way she and Kyle could make their thoughts known to one another. Communication on such a deep level is rare. Or at least that's what I thought, until people started telling me stories about the Whippets they adopted from me.

CHAPTER 6

THE HEALING POWER OF WHIPPETS

JON AND JEAN MENDRES came out to my Whippet kennel one December and introduced their nine-year-old daughter, Amber. Amber was slight and blonde, with sparkling hazel eyes. They were a busy family. Jon was an earnest police officer; Jean worked tirelessly for abused children in her job at New Jersey's Division of Youth and Family Services; Amber excelled in her schoolwork. Their son, Sean, required lots of extra care because he'd been born with a developmental disability. The family were devoted animal lovers. Jean and Amber trained their horses and trailered them to shows on weekends to compete.

Amber wanted a dog of her own. She'd done the research and chosen a Whippet, which was a good choice for the sensitive, considerate child she was. When she looked among a scrambling, scurrying litter of two-month-old puppies, she fell in love with a black brindle and white male, whom she named Cisco. As we talked, the kennel door opened and Sean walked in, a blond, freckled, seemingly unhappy teenager.

"Can we go now?" he asked.

Jean patiently explained that they were discussing the new puppy for Amber. It would take a few more minutes. He crossed his arms against his chest.

"Would you like to hold one of the puppies?" I suggested.

"I hate puppies," he said. He slouched into a chair.

"You don't hate puppies," Jean said, but Sean then replied, "Yes, I do." His tone and aspect were that of a much younger child.

Jean smiled at me, so we continued the lesson with Amber. How to pick the right puppy, how to take care of it, things the new puppy would need. Amber was an avid student. She wanted to know everything.

There was a six-month-old puppy in the room with us, one that Amber hadn't seen because he was hiding under the sofa. He was white with a red saddle and mask. All seven other members of his litter had been sold. But no one had picked out Captain to take home as their pet. He was not an outgoing puppy. When people came to visit, other puppies rushed them, wanting to be first to be hugged and held. Not Captain. He hung back, curling up and nodding off to sleep by himself. Sometimes I'd put him into someone's arms, to make sure he was socialized. But as soon as he was lowered to the ground, he'd go off by himself, choosing no one.

When Amber and her family came in, I let Captain out of his run and into the room with us. He promptly went to sleep under a chair.

Now, out of the corner of my eye, I saw that Captain had come out from under the sofa and was staring at Sean. Sean ignored him. I expected Captain to crawl right back, but an amazing thing happened. Captain approached Sean, and put a paw on his knee.

My voice kept on talking to Amber, but I was shocked. Captain had never before shown any interest in anyone. He'd had so little contact with people that I wasn't sure what he'd do.

Sean said to Captain, "Go away!"

His mother looked over and put a finger to her lips, asking Sean not to yell. Sean shook his head.

Instead of going away, Captain stood up and put both feet on Sean, who continued to ignore him. Then, he gave a little jump and boosted himself onto Sean's lap. From there, he crawled up so his paws were on Sean's shoulder.

Sean yelled, "Get this dog off me!"

"This is very odd," I said. "That's Captain, and he doesn't like anybody. He's always in this room, but he hides. He's never come out before." I pulled him off Sean and returned him to the floor. Then I asked the Mendres family to come down the aisle to a run where they could meet the sire of Amber's puppy. That gave Captain a little time to try to win over Sean.

Sure enough, once again, Captain went to Sean; the dog hoisted himself up until he was lying across Sean's chest. Again, this was very odd. I pointed out to Jean and Jon that Captain had arranged himself so that his heart was lying exactly over Sean's heart. I'd never seen anything like this. "Is there something wrong with Sean's heart?" I asked.

Jon and Jean exchanged a look of apprehension. Jean said that Sean had a neurological impairment. There was no exact diagnosis for his condition.

My biggest worry was that Sean might push the puppy and injure him. But as we watched, Sean showed no inclination to do that. He reluctantly put an arm on Captain so he wouldn't fall. But when he saw us looking at him, he called out, "Get this dog off me!"

As I took Captain from Sean, I told him about the dog. How

he was born in a litter with four brothers and three sisters. How all of them had found families and were gone. How the others had liked to roughhouse together and tumble all day, but Captain never liked to play this way. He preferred to be quiet and aloof. Sean was the first person he'd ever noticed.

As the Mendres prepared to leave, I told them that I would never urge anyone to get a dog they didn't want, but that the interaction between Captain and Sean was something special.

Sean then asked, "Why can't I get a dog, too?"

The family said they needed to talk about this new development as they initially were only in the market for one puppy. They understood that two puppies would be a lot of work. And they weren't sure Sean was ready for the responsibility. They said they would think about it.

The files on all the dogs were nearby. I wanted to check on Captain's age. I said, "He's six months old. He was born July 23."

Sean said excitedly, "That's almost the same as my birthday! July 21."

That little fact sealed the deal. Captain went home with Sean. They left the kennel with Captain in Sean's arms.

From the start, Captain gave Sean something he'd never had before: a best friend. Sean's developmental disabilities had made it all but impossible for him to establish ties with people. But he had no trouble forming a bond with Captain. Sean was proud to have a dog who thought he was so special. He was normally silent, so the teachers at school were surprised to hear him talking. He was describing the special dog who liked only him. The amount of talking he was doing was exciting to all. And Captain was the stimulus. It was clear to everyone that the two were a team.

Jean kept in touch with me. She shared the news that Sean, who had never wanted to go to school, take part in any activity, or get any exercise, changed into a different boy. He kept up a running commentary of life, directed at Captain. Captain, who had previously avoided all other humans, listened intently to every word. Captain slept curled into Sean's chest. Sean walked and fed him, more responsibility than he'd shown before. He liked playing fetch with Captain and telling other people about him.

Fifteen years later, Amber is now studying for an advanced degree in child psychology. She has a special gift for working with children with autism and mental retardation. The Whippet she got from me all those years ago, Cisco, has just passed on, and is much missed.

Sean is doing well. You can't quantify the positive effect Captain had on him. But with his steady presence and his insistence on loving only Sean, he definitely helped him. He came into Sean's life when he was an angry, resentful child and helped him to grow out of that place. He made Sean feel important, like a person who really mattered.

Now, Captain's health is failing. Five times in the last two years, veterinarians warned Jean to say good-bye, because his heart problems were getting worse. But each time, Captain pulled through, to return to his place at Sean's side. Jean worries about the effect Captain's death will have on Sean. But Sean has shown strength and understanding toward this inevitable event. When Cisco died, Sean consoled Jean by saying: "Don't cry, Mom. He's in a better place."

⌒

NORMAN BARTON HAD owned Whippets since the 1920s, and he loved this svelte breed. When his last dog died, Norman's son, Jack, drove him to my kennel from his home on Lake Hopatcong, New Jersey. Norman used a cane. It was difficult for him to get around. And he had no interest in life without a Whippet. Delighted with a mostly white puppy, Norman named him Willie after his favorite country and western singer. Jack lived in Virginia, but visited his father and Willie often. He promised to take Willie to the veterinarian for his shots and worming. And Norman had neighbors who offered to help in an emergency. Once again, he could enjoy the dignified company of a sighthound.

Norman understood that a young Whippet was also a rowdy animal. I was worried that the puppy might not get enough discipline or housetraining, but Norman managed it. The situation worked well despite my trepidation. Until Norman had a stroke. Jack told me his father was recovering well, but Willie had become anxious and uncontrollable. Without Norman and a regular daily routine, he was no longer housetrained and was chewing the furniture and curtains.

There were no dogs allowed in the hospital where Norman was being treated. But Jack was handsome and charming, and he convinced the night nurse to open the fire exit door so he could bring Willie in. When Willie finally saw Norman, all the angry, destructive energy went out of him. He leaped onto Norman's bed and lay by his side. Norman stroked and whispered to him. Willie didn't stir. Jack and the night nurse teared up at the potent emotion between the old man and the dog.

Jack put Willie in a kennel for a few weeks while his father went through rehabilitation. Jack also had to sell Norman's house and moved his things in with him at his condo in Alexandria. He got Norman settled on the first floor with a bathroom for the disabled and easy access from the kitchen to the living room to the front door. When Jack brought Willie home from the boarding kennel, Norman was sitting on the sofa, wearing his old trucker's cap and watching TV. The dog took one look at Norman and made a leap from the doorway to the sofa in a long, deerlike arc. He snatched the cap off Norman's head and did three laps around the living room with it, then brought it back to Norman's lap.

The doctors told Jack that Norman's heart was failing, telling him he didn't have much longer to live. Jack wanted to keep his father at home, but the day he came home from work and found Norman passed out, he panicked and called an ambulance. In the hospital, doctors were unable to resuscitate Norman. They didn't think he'd last through the night. But he did, and the next night, too. Norman wasn't conscious, but Jack sensed he was uncomfortable.

Once again, he got together with a night nurse and got her to open the fire exit door. He brought Willie to his father's room. Willie covered Norman's face with kisses, then nuzzled his neck and lay down with his head on Norman's shoulder. Jack watched his father's hand, which had barely moved for the past two days, lift shakily to touch the dog.

Jack and Willie stayed until midnight. Willie refused to leave. Jack had to peel him off the bed. He whispered in his father's ear: "Goodnight, Dad. Willie and I are going home. We're going to watch TV and have a beer. We'll be waiting for you." Maybe it was his imagination, but Jack thought that the troubled look on his father's face had changed. His father now appeared tranquil and at peace.

When he got back to the condo, the phone was ringing. It was the hospital. His father had died. Jack is not an emotional person, but he sat down on the sofa and hugged Willie for an hour. For once, wild Willie was quiet. He let Jack hold him.

Jack felt he'd done the right thing, bringing Willie to the hospital to say good-bye. Even though his father hadn't spoken, Jack felt that he had fulfilled his father's last wish. His father had wanted Willie there in his final hours.

HARVEY ZANE'S WIFE warned him not to get a dog. She didn't think he'd remember to feed it and exercise it, and she didn't want the responsibility. But Harvey admired the photos of the purebred Whippet in his co-worker's cubicle. He'd never had a dog before, but he felt a dog would be a good addition to his life, especially an exotic one. He knew he was supposed to get more exercise and spend more time outdoors. Maybe if he had a dog, he would do so.

His co-worker, Nancy, warned him that Whippets were expensive, but he decided to call me anyway.

Nancy was a good friend of mine, so I was happy to show my puppies to someone she recommended. She was a little hesitant about Norman's qualifications. But as she saw him every day, she could monitor the situation.

At my house, the dozens of framed photos of champions and racers, and the many trophies that graced my living room, impressed Norman. He loved the dogs who pushed up to him to say hello. But he wasn't interested in a squirming litter of eight-week-old puppies, whose prices started at $650.

There was a mostly white, older puppy in the group greeting Harvey who we called Hammer. Hammer had the Whippet's elegant outline and dark eyes, but he would never have a career in the show ring because he was a monorchid. Show dogs are required to have two normally descended testicles, but one of Hammer's had been retained. This meant he could not compete in AKC show or coursing or racing events. And people who came to buy pet puppies were passing him over, perhaps because he was missing dark pigment around one of his eyes, which made him look like a pirate.

But Harvey didn't notice this "flaw." He saw only Hammer's good qualities, his strong muscles, arched neck, and happy attitude. When I told him he could have Hammer for a $100 adoption fee, he looked at me in disbelief. I lent him a collar and leash so he could take Hammer home.

Both Nancy and I were anxious about selling him to Harvey and were prepared to take the dog back if it didn't work out. But despite his wife's dire prediction, Harvey bonded immediately with Hammer and made his care a priority in his life. From the very first day together, the pair's long walks became part of their routine. Harvey's extra belly fat started to tighten up. His blood pressure lowered. His overall health improved.

Harvey's cardiologist was skeptical about giving Hammer any credit, but Harvey felt his dog was a good influence. He particularly enjoyed the looks they received when they were out on their walks. People often asked what breed of dog Hammer was and admired his elegance. Harvey, of course, thought Hammer was the most beautiful dog in the world and told everyone so. He usually added that by hard bargaining he had managed to get Hammer at the discount price of a hundred dollars, which truly impressed people who knew the prices of purebred dogs.

Harvey's wife, Judith, was secretly pleased that the dog had had such a positive influence on her husband. She left the two of them alone and stayed out of their relationship.

Then, Judith became stricken with breast cancer. She underwent extensive treatment that left her exhausted. She had to stop working and spent most days in bed. Hammer decided she needed company, and stretched out by her side. The body of a Whippet is very warm; it is warmer than many other breeds due to a low percentage of body fat. Hammer felt like a heating pad against her back.

The cancer treatments kept Judith alive for another year, but it was a difficult one. She didn't feel well most of the time. She had little appetite and looked frail. Harvey wished he could stay home all day with her, but he had to work to remain qualified for the health insurance Judith needed. But he felt happy knowing that Hammer was there, looking out for her, keeping her warm, giving her strength with his stalwart presence.

⌣⟩

EVEN THOUGH I AM presently a Whippet breeder, Brussels Griffons have been with me since my college days. As "Griffies" weigh only 10 pounds, one of these pint-sized characters is usually tucked into a bag on my shoulder that looks deceptively like a purse. When I decided to show and breed Griffies, I discovered that Brussels Griffon aficionados are as convinced of the healing power of their breed as Whippet fanatics are about theirs. Take Cara Pellegrini, for example.

She sat across the kitchen table from me recently, her big eyes shining as she played with two Brussels Griffon puppies. Cara has short black hair that swings bouncily as she talks. Her arms are completely covered with tattoos, so that it's hard to tell if she has a shirt on or if you are looking at her skin.

She clutched one little seven-week-old Brussels Griffon puppy to her chest as the other draped itself across her foot. She explained why she went to the trouble of tracking down a Brussels Griffon breeder like me; it's because her Affenpinscher, Spider, needs a friend. She wants another little dog as sort of a companion for her companion, so when she's at work, the two dogs can keep each other company.

Cara was trying to decide which of these two puppies she would take with her, when they were ready to leave home in a few weeks. The dark-faced one or the light-faced? Both were sweet, friendly, outgoing, happy, and darling. But the light-faced boy caught her attention. She's the manager of a restaurant, working extra shifts as a bartender to pay for the puppy. Last night, behind the bar, a giant bottle of Jack Daniels whiskey slipped out of her grasp and landed on her big toe. A liter bottle. It was full. The force of the weight bent the toenail and loosened it; tiny blood vessels were squashed and ruptured and today the injury is purple, swollen, and throbbing. It is difficult to walk. It hurt so much she thought of calling to cancel her visit, but she was too eager to see the new puppies.

What she wanted me to know was that the light-faced puppy had discovered her injury and was concerned. Every time she put him on the floor, he immediately went to the swollen toe and licked it. She thinks he is trying to help her.

This isn't the first time she's noticed the healing urge of a small dog. Her Affenpinscher acts the same way.

"He loves going everywhere that I go. We'd go over to my Mom's house and he'd say hello to everybody, but mostly he sat with me.

"My grandmother wasn't doing well. She started to get Alzheimer's. She looked pretty much the same to everybody else, but Spider knew there was something wrong with her. One day, he went over and cuddled up next to her. He'd never done that before. She started petting him, and said: 'Hello, Blackie! Good boy.' She thought he was a dog she had sixty years ago, when she was a little girl.

"It was as if he knew that his presence would help her. She was calm when he was around. He connected her to good things in her life."

Cara picked up the puppy and stroked him. "He knows my toe hurts and he's trying to help me," she said.

Who's to say she's wrong? There are many people who claim that their dogs seem intuitively to be therapists. Some dogs make a hopeless situation bearable. Some dogs are so good at this that people think they are angels or spiritual beings sent from God. For some people, dogs can provide more consistent emotional support than any of their human relatives or friends. That thought was at the heart of a groundbreaking organization in San Francisco called Pets Are Wonderful Support. They went to great lengths to prove it.

CHAPTER 7

PETS ARE WONDERFUL SUPPORT

IN 1986, THERE WERE more than 500 charitable organizations in San Francisco where generous people could volunteer their time. Sara decided to help out at the food bank, because their mission crossed many categories, including the sick and homeless and children and the elderly. On Saturday mornings, she'd spend several hours at the cold and poorly lit warehouse, unpacking flats of Rice Krispies and stacking shelves with English muffins and Wheat Thins. On Tuesday evenings, she helped make up food bundles and hand them out at St. Dominic's.

She particularly liked talking with the elderly clients about their lives and the services they received. She came from a middle-class family and graduated from the University of San Francisco. She'd never been poor and hungry, and she had a lot of sympathy in her heart for people who were less fortunate. Her social life revolved around her boyfriend and her Golden Retriever, Rambo. She worked for a firm that designed microelectronics. So she was happy to spend some time talking about good doctors and ungrateful children and loved and lost careers, rather than transistors, capacitors, inductors, resistors, and diodes.

One day a frail elderly woman in a ragged pink sweater tugged on her sleeve and asked if she could please have some Dinty Moore Beef Stew. Sara did a brief search, but the food bank didn't have that product this week. The woman, Ruth, balked at the idea of canned chili. So Sara helped her locate Bumblebee tuna fish and Hormel Spam.

"That's good you're getting plenty of protein," Sara said approvingly.

"Oh, it's not for me," Ruth whispered. "It's for Harry."

"Your husband?"

"My dog."

At first, Sara smiled. They chatted about Harry, whom Ruth said was a white Miniature Poodle she'd had for twelve years. But later, Sara turned the conversation over in her mind, and began to wonder how many of the food bank clients were giving their food to their dogs. A client got only a set amount to take home, an amount calculated to be enough to keep them from starvation in case they had no other source of food. If Ruth was feeding hers to Harry, it might be why she looked so frail and unhealthy.

Casual conversations with the other food bank clients confirmed her fears. All of them shared their food with their pets. They were more than happy to tell her so.

At first, Sara tried suggesting they give the pets to relatives or friends or let one of the adoption agencies help them find the pet a home. But she quickly gave up that line of conversation. People were horrified. No matter how sick or frail, they told her they would never give up Sam or Max or Bear. They would never let Buddy or Maggie or Chelsea go hungry. Brandy and Ginger and Taffy were their best friends.

These sick and elderly people were ignoring their own nutritional needs in order to give food to their pets. The food bank did not supply pet food, so the dogs and cats were eating the Chef Boyardee Spaghetti & Meatballs, Campbell's Chicken Soup, and Honey Glazed Ham meant for the ailing clients.

No amount of coercion could convince these people that their dogs didn't need the food as much as they did. Clearly, something should be done. A group of the volunteers had already locked onto the problem and determined to do something about it.

First, the volunteers approached the companies who donated the canned peas and evaporated milk and applesauce. But those executives demurred at the idea of supplying food for pets. Their charity was directed towards basic human staples. When they murmured that pets were a luxury item, they were simply mirroring the culture's thoughts on the matter. Asking donors to supply pet food to the poor seemed like an unnecessary burden.

The volunteers realized that they didn't agree. Down here on the streets, where they had day-to-day contact with the sick and disabled, they came to see that a pet was not the extravagance the distributors thought it was. Many of these people were disconnected from their nuclear families, either through death or rejection. The dog was their only source of love. It was the only creature they cared for other than themselves. The dog was a stable presence in their lives. If you took the dog away, you were taking away structure and discipline, something ill people need but often can't organize for themselves. The dog was not a social parasite, preying on the owner's goodwill and giving nothing in return. They offered their owners raw, unfiltered, and unconditional love, trust, and respect. They took the patient's mind off his troubles and onto a being outside of himself. Unlike people, with whom interactions may be complex and unpredictable, dogs provide a constant source of comfort. It was time for charities to realize that.

This was revolutionary thinking in 1986. They didn't get a lot of support.

Their first move was to convince the food bank to carry pet food and pet-related products. The idea went up the chain of command, and those in charge at the food bank listened. They made an effort to get some dog and cat food. But their hearts weren't in it, because it had nothing to do with their real work. Their goal was to fill the stomachs of people, not their animals.

That's how PAWS got started, by a group of volunteers who realized that a person's pet might be his lifeline. Most of the volunteers had their own pets. They wouldn't want to be without them, and didn't think others should be made to do without them, either.

They came up with the acronym PAWS–Pets Are Wonderful Support. The names of people in the initial group who founded PAWS in 1986 seem to be lost to history. Their work started a wonderful organization, but they didn't spend time eulogizing themselves because of it. They spread the word to others, like Sara, who was happy to volunteer for such a new and worthy cause.

The early PAWS was a sort of grassroots storefront organization. They set up a pet food bank, where people could pick up dog and cat food, special diets, kitty litter, flea treatments, dog shampoo, and other pet-related items. Soon, they had volunteers driving around in their own cars to deliver a month's supply of food to people who were too sick to make it to the building.

After a few years of observing San Francisco's most needy inhabitants, another idea occurred to them. While supplying food was a great idea, maybe it didn't quite go far enough. Some of the most desperate situations didn't call for food. They needed another kind of help, and unless they got it, chances were that the pet would end up in the animal shelter. Take, for example, the plight of an English Springer Spaniel named Mattie, who was stuck alone in a Castro district townhouse because her owner had been taken to the hospital.

Mattie belonged to a computer programmer named Ken, who had moved to San Francisco from the Midwest. The city suited his lifestyle better than the old-fashioned farming town in which he'd grown up. His parents had been expecting grandchildren for so long that Ken eventually revealed to them that he was gay. They were not happy to hear it. A gay son had never been part of their plans. Family relations were severed. They had not spoken to Ken for five years.

So when Ken was struck by a strange and terrifying illness called AIDS, there was no one to comfort him, except his dog. This was the late eighties, a time when the ranks of gay men were being decimated by AIDS. There was little known about it, few doctors who could treat it, and few medicines that could fight its disabling effects. The rapidity with which a diagnosis of HIV-positive could turn into full-blown AIDS was frightening. Today, there are better treatments that can extend the life of many, but it is still an unnerving illness. It is terrifying for couples, but it may be even more overwhelming when the sick person must face it alone.

Ken often felt as if he was fighting a bad case of flu, with headaches, exhaustion, and chills that would turn into sweats. His throat was coated with white spots and he had painful sores on both legs. He lost a lot of weight. When he stayed home from work, Mattie lay down next to him, and he was grateful for the company. When he shivered with a wash of chills, she snuggled in even closer.

The virus had entered his system and was busily penetrating his healthy white cells. After never ending doctors' visits and an ever growing fistful of pills, after exhaustion and diarrhea, after painful shingles across his ribs and day after day with 101 degree fever, a friend from the GLBT Center found Ken in his home, almost unconscious. When an ambulance was summoned to take him away, Ken was too weak to protest. Once in the hospital, treatment for dehydration started to restore him, and as soon as he could talk, he only wanted to know one thing—where was Mattie?

An AIDS volunteer got a phone call through to the friend from the Center. It turned out that he'd left Mattie at the house and was going over when he could after work to let her out and feed her. When Ken heard that, he tried to unhook himself from the IV drips and get out of there. He couldn't let Mattie be alone, getting outside only once in awhile. A nurse convinced him he was too weak to leave, but it was hard to listen to medical advice when all he could think of was his dog.

His GLBT friend picked up food for Mattie at the PAWS pet food bank, where he told Sara, one of the volunteers, the sad story of the lonely English Springer Spaniel, waiting in the house for a man who might or might not return. Sara lived in the same neighborhood. She offered to help with feeding and walking in the evening. She enlisted her mother to walk Mattie in the morning.

Mattie was sweet and affectionate and cooperated with whoever came to walk her. Sara took a Polaroid photo of Mattie sitting in Ken's easy chair, and wrote in Magic Marker, "When are you coming home?" She took it to San Francisco General, where doctors had discovered that pneumocystis pneumonia had turned Ken's system into its own private factory. They had a new experimental drug to fight it, trimethoprim-sulfamethoxazole, which was working well on other AIDS patients. Doctors were hoping TMP-SMX would let Ken's body build up CD4+ T cells and lower the rate of colonization, which was nearing 60 percent. But it didn't seem to be working. Ken's body showed no response to the antibiotic—until Sara's visit.

When Sara told him that Mattie was fine, she was being walked and brushed and fed, and was eager for him to come home, something altered in Ken's chemistry. For four days he'd shown absolutely no response to drug therapy. The morning after Sara's visit, his red blood cell count started to rise, and his viral load began to drop. Maybe it was the good care at San Francisco General. Maybe his body had needed a certain saturation of TMP-SMX. Maybe it was just coincidence. But when Ken heard that someone was taking good care of Mattie, that she was well and waiting for him, it rekindled his will to live. It took several weeks, but he was eventually able to leave the hospital and return home.

Sara and her mother continued to walk Mattie because Ken was too weak to do it. When Sara's mother took off for three days for a holiday weekend in Reno, Sara asked around at the PAWS pet food bank for someone to help her. Three people enlisted. This meant that each person could come every other day, which was much less of a burden.

The PAWS people heard about another man in much the same predicament, and organized a team of volunteers to care for his German Shepherd. Then they set up a group of four to take temporary custody of another man's Yorkshire Terrier.

PAWS saw a need, and plunged wholeheartedly into the business of helping very ill people keep their pets. They suspected something that would later be proven by researchers who kept records and measured blood pressure: for some people, owning a dog is better medicine than all the AIDS drugs in the world.

The current president of PAWS, John Lipp, says of that time, "PAWS was seen as a warm and fuzzy, expendable thing. We were trying to tell people, we are not expendable. This is an important mission."

The organization gained ground throughout the next decade. The world was becoming an increasingly impersonal place. Instead of trips to the bank or the clothing store, connecting with other humans, more and more people stayed home and did their shopping and communicating on the Internet. As a corollary, many people deepened their relationships with their dogs, seeing them more as family and friends then simply pets. Dogs were good comforters and excellent listeners. They offered their owners unconditional love and support. One of those people was Randy Allgaier.

Randy Allgaier is tall, slim, redheaded, and walks with a long stride that speaks of a forthright and determined approach to life. He lives at the top of a hill in San Francisco's Castro neighborhood, a hill so steep his friends groan when he issues dinner invitations. It's a hill that's daunting to more hesitant humans, but Randy's quick walk swallows it up. Usually, his redheaded, solidly built Beagle, Darwin, is by his side.

For many years, Randy worked in public policy, for the nonprofit San Francisco AIDS Foundation, and the state's AIDS Drug Assistance Program and the national Human Rights Campaign. He was a tireless organizer of community demonstrations and large fundraising events. His efforts benefited millions of Californians. Thousands of citizens will never get HIV or AIDS because Randy's efforts convinced the state to pay for education on how to prevent AIDS transmission and for clean needles for addicts. Although illness is a highly personal matter, the people he helped will never know his name.

At around the time he turned forty, Randy unfortunately faced some terrible prospects. Stretched to the limit by his busy job, his HIV-positive status turned into full-blown AIDS. After hospitalization, he was bedridden for many weeks. His partner, Lee, was gone during the day at his stressful job teaching adults with mental disabilities. Randy was alone, except for the company of his dog, Darwin. Darwin, a Beagle, was always a happy and entertaining presence. But while Randy was sick, he noticed something unusual about Darwin, who was usually most concerned about his own needs to go outside or get a walk or be petted and acknowledged. "He knew I was sick, and didn't leave my side. Darwin is a creature of habit, but he altered his habit to lie in bed with me all day long. He had this look in his eyes that felt like he knew there was something wrong. And that he was saying, 'I'm here with you.' He was a great comfort. With Darwin there, I didn't feel I was alone."

As he recovered, Randy realized with deep regret that in order to care for his health, he would have to leave his job. Lee extracted a promise that for the first six months of his retirement, he would make health his number-one priority and not work for any organization. For Randy, that was a big promise as he was almost compulsive about jumping in to help wherever he saw need.

With time and space to recover, Randy's health started to improve. He gives Darwin some of the credit as he helped refocus Randy's energy. While Randy was honoring his promise not to organize any community events, Lee hadn't placed any ban on attending them, so the two dog lovers wound up at Petchitecture, a unique cocktail party that attracts 1,000 people with about 500 dogs every May. Prominent architects and designers build pet habitats that are on view and later auctioned off. The event raises a lot of money, and the funds go to an organization Randy was curious about, Pets Are Wonderful Support.

Randy said, "It was a small organization, but this fundraiser was huge. And they put it on themselves. I was impressed by that."

He was also impressed with PAWS's unique mission to keep people with disabling illnesses together with their pets. Randy was so impressed by PAWS that the day after the six-month agreement with Lee was over, he wrote a letter to the board president and executive director and offered his help. "Having had the experience of Darwin when I was very sick," he said, "their mission statement spoke to my heart in ways that were very important."

The people at PAWS recognized a kindred spirit. A month later, Randy was on their board, and four months later, he was the PAWS board president.

"Darwin is a key reason I got involved. It was a passion about their mission that had me so driving and motivated. I got it at the most basic level. It wasn't abstract. I knew it."

During the four years that Randy Allgaier was president, he secured big donors who not only could keep PAWS going, but give sufficient funding to enlarge PAWS's mission. Randy also knew how to entice smaller donors to put this charity on their yearly "Donations" list. And the gods were smiling; a check for $900,000 simply showed up in the mail at the PAWS office one day. A skeptical Randy warned the others: "Don't celebrate until it clears the bank." But it did, and another $200,000 eventually followed. Randy discovered both donations had come from a woman who had heard about the organization's mission shortly before her death. He still shakes his head over that piece of good luck. The PAWS budget doubled.

PAWS also created a program for the dogs of the homeless. Randy says he was surprised at first that these people did not rejoice at the chance to have their dogs neutered and spayed for free. "There is so little in their life they have control over, but that is one of the areas they do. But over time, if you kind of gently work with them, they'll do it. But when you first ask, they balk." Randy was an excellent caretaker of the PAWS mission. He took them from a small organization to one with a $3-million-dollar annual budget. He feels good when someone points out that his work at PAWS has kept thousands of people together with their dogs. But Randy is of the strong opinion that a non-profit organization like PAWS needs to refresh itself constantly with new management. So after four years as president, he ceded the role to someone else.

⌐⌐

IN APRIL 2007, on a cool Saturday morning, the downtown office buildings of the South of Market neighborhood of San Francisco are largely deserted. Cars are free to wander up and down the steep hills, and even turn around in the middle of the block. The workers who keep the place humming all week are at home.

At 645 Harrison Street, a nondescript warehouse and office building, a quiet group gathers at the front door. Only a small sign in a window indicates that the organization PAWS works here. Just before ten, the door swings open and a smiling young man with dark hair waves everyone in. He is greeted with cries of "Prado!" "How you doin'?" and "Como esta?" These people are PAWS clients, and they've come to take advantage of the weekly pet food bank.

In the back of the building, cars and pickup trucks are pulling up to the loading dock: an older white Ford F-150 with a rusted cargo bed, a battered yellow Volkswagen Beetle, a silver Lexus RX polished to a gleaming shine, and other vehicles that spoke volumes about the fact that PAWS was a charity supported by people throughout the economic spectrum, rich and poor, young and old.

An intern working with Prado, a freshman from the Midwest named Elena, is getting college credit from San Francisco State by putting in hours of work here. They pack the foods onto pallets for each driver. Together they wheel out boxes of Friskies and Milkbones, Iams and Natural Choice, Veterinary Diet and Blue Seal kibble.

The volunteers work in pairs, necessary in San Francisco where very often the driver is not going to find a place to park. The driver pulls up to the address and either puts on the flashing lights or circles the block. The runner carries the food up the steep steps of San Francisco hillside homes or into the rattling elevators of low-income housing.

One driver, Janis, just smiles when she is asked why she gives up two hours on a Saturday morning to drive dog food around the city. She is an Asian American who used to work in the HIV field at a medical firm. Driving for PAWS makes her feel that she is still doing something useful to combat the disease. Her runner, Maria, works for a company that puts movies on cellphones. "Because of how I feel about Buster—that's my dog—I know how these people feel," Maria says. "There's nothing more important than knowing that your dog is going to get fed. If I was sick, I'd want someone to do this for me."

Joan's runner is her fifteen-year-old daughter, Cameron. They stack bags of kibble into the rear cargo section of their car with the easy camaraderie of those who have done this before. "It's about volunteerism," Joan answers, as to why she helps PAWS. "If all I did was tell her that it's a good thing to help out in the community, they would be empty words. This way, we get to spend Saturday mornings together, which is kind of nice."

Inside the building, in a large area in front of the offices, Prado is shaking a bag full of collars into a cardboard box. He attaches a sign, FREE COLLARS, and watches as the people who come to pick up the dog food carefully measure and compare. A transvestite asks, "Does this pink color clash with Shandalay's coat? Do you think I should take the green one?" Prado votes for the green one. Several patrons gather round to give her fashion advice. She really wants her Bichon mix to sport the pink one. Eventually the group approves that decision and she leaves, smiling. Another man winds a collar onto the neck of his 6-pound, long-suffering Chihuahua, who sighs to let everyone know what he puts up with.

Various people sit around in the hard-backed chairs of the PAWS waiting room. It's easy to see that this is an important time for them to socialize. Everyone who comes in greets Prado heartily. His smile and obvious good nature make everyone his friend, even a heavy, white-haired, older woman who has only been here once before and is not sure where she put her blue card. Prado tells her gently that he needs the card; it is the emblem of her acceptance into the PAWS program. He'll need to date stamp it when he gives her the food. She takes a seat and sorts through the contents of her purse. Here it is! Her black Labrador, Birdie, will eat for another month, although the size of Birdie's waist means it's been a long time since she's missed a meal.

One by one, the clients show up, some excitedly, some hesitantly, always with their dogs. Prado bestows a big, welcoming smile on each one, which puts an imprimatur on their acceptance and leads to conversations with other members of the group. One guess what everyone is talking about: They are debating the merits of Pit Bulls versus Boxers; giving each other advice on how to calm a Jack Russell or get a Bulldog out for a walk; relating what the vet said about Holly's itchy spot during their latest visit to Pets Unlimited.

The next person into the building is a slim and gentlemanly veterinarian, Dr. Durfee. He's retired from twenty-eight years of treating small pets in Fresno. He was born in San Francisco and always planned on coming back. He's not here to give medical care; everyone in San Francisco knows that the Pets Unlimited, the SPCA Animal Hospital, and VetSOS treat the dogs of low-income and homeless persons. Dr. Durfee is going to cut nails, a simple and necessary undertaking that is quite beyond many of these people. They are happy to form a semi-orderly line and wait to enter a small conference room that has been turned into a treatment bay.

A young woman with a very loud voice comes in and announces that everyone needs to stand aside, "A big mean dog is coming in here and he'll tear all of your dogs to bits." Everybody grabs their own dogs and holds them close. A jaunty mauve beret comes into view atop the head of a small, bent and frail woman. Out in front of her, barking as loud as possible, marches a black and white Boston Terrier. Everyone gives a little laugh. This is the vicious dog? They decide, with the urging of the young woman, to let Beanie in at the front of the line to be the next one to see the vet, wisely figuring that the sooner that loud bark and bad reputation are out of the room, the better.

The march into the inner office produces, a moment later, a terrible scream. Beanie has bitten the vet.

Dr. Durfee comes out with his handkerchief wrapped around his hand. Blood is seeping through. "That's bad," he diagnoses. He shakes his head in wonder. "Bitten by a little Boston Terrier," he muses. "I haven't been bitten in twenty years. And the funny thing is, he didn't even need his nails cut."

A bald man who owns Chico, a shepherd-Labrador mix, says, "He just came in to bite the vet!"

The troop in the waiting area cracks up. They encompass a diverse compendium of dog lovers. There are all the same types you would see in any veterinarian's outer office or at a public dog park. The Pretty Girl, stroking her silky Shih Tzu and bragging to anyone who will listen that Gemma's parents are champions. The Angry Guy, who is angry when he comes in, confirmed in his anger when he hears the supply of Science Diet has run out, and angry when he leaves, clutching a bag of Blue Seal, his mixed-breed terrier hurrying at his side. The Very Bad Dog Trainer, whose idea of good dog control is to give his wild Pit Bull twelve feet of leash so he can charge at everyone in every direction. He doesn't notice that people snatch up their own dogs when his wild one approaches. He is occupied with smiling at Lance's behavior. Soon all the small dogs have been picked up to where Lance can't get at them, and the big dogs are being forcibly restrained from turning Lance into lunch. All the diversity of the canine world, all the madness of the human one.

The volunteers come from all walks of life. Ellen Sinaiko runs a restaurant called La Méditerranée in the Castro district. It's a busy job, but she makes time in her day to care for the beloved mixed breed of a man with AIDS, and has dashed out many times to get a sick dog to a vet. Slight Anne Marie Harper laughs that she needs the exercise, so she takes a big Shar-Pei/Mastiff mix, Chango, for long hikes up and down the Portrero streets. Grace Walker has been walking Angel, a black-and-white terrier mix, for eight years, the devotion of both of them keeping a sick owner going from day to day.

PAWS SF distributes 700 cans of wet food and 900 pounds of dry food each week to about 500 clients. Each month, the group accepts twenty new applicants who have heard about it by word of mouth, or at a vet clinic, or from a social worker. When new clients get in, they gain access to the pet food bank and can get help with dog-walking. But maybe the most important benefit is the peace of knowing that if they ever find themselves facing emergency hospitalization, a good-hearted volunteer—someone like Prado or Elena or Janis or Sara—will step in and provide temporary foster care for their animals. PAWS clients, all of whom live with a disabling illness and on an income of less than $950 a month, are able to maintain the irreplaceable bond with their pets. Their animal companions are not dropped at the door of an already overburdened shelter system.

The people at PAWS wanted the worlds of science and medicine to prove that keeping sick people together with their dogs was giving them better health and longer lives. They formed a partnership with the vet school at University of California/Davis to look at the impact of animals on people who have AIDS. They joined forces with Dr. Lynette Hart, a professor and researcher who has a great interest in exploring the human-canine bond. Dr. Hart helped to establish, in 1985, the Center for Animals in Society (CAS), which was among the first organizations to study the human-canine bond. PAWS and Dr. Hart were a perfect match.

When PAWS began its mission in 1987, it was the only "human-animal support service" in the country. As the pioneer, PAWS invented its mission and solved problems as it went along. PAWS recognized that something in the human-canine bond had shifted, and it was among the first to acknowledge the new role of dogs in human lives. But the group wasn't alone for long. There was a groundswell in this kind of thinking, particularly in California. Just 50 miles north, in the Sonoma Valley town of Santa Rosa, a schoolteacher named Bonnie Bergin made an amazing discovery that would change the relationship between humans and canines in ways that would reverberate all around the globe.

CHAPTER 8

BONNIE BERGIN
AND THE AMAZING
POWER OF DOGS

NORTHERN CALIFORNIA'S Sonoma County is known for its thermal springs, redwood forests, ocean beaches, quaint towns, vineyards, and wineries. Vacationers tour through the towns of Healdsburg, Petaluma, Guerneville, and Geyserville, stopping at Clos du Bois, Gallo, Geyser Peak, Kendall-Jackson, St. Francis, and Simi wineries for sips of estate reserve Cabernet, Petite Sirah, Claret, Merlot, and Zinfandel.

Nestled in the center of the county is its largest city, Santa Rosa. For a small but intense group of people, Santa Rosa is the region's most important destination. They are people who travel in wheelchairs or on crutches or who have little use of their arms. They head for one particular block of Santa Rosa that is known locally as "service-dog row."

The Sebastopol Road neighborhood is home to the headquarters of a cluster of organizations—Canine Companions for Independence, Assistance Dogs International, the SFSPCA's Hearing Dog Program, Guide Dogs, Loving Paws Assistance Dogs, and the only educational institution in the world that grants a degree in service dog training: the Assistance Dog Institute.

The institute is housed in several nondescript tan buildings set amid stands of eucalyptus trees. The first thing a visitor notices is the dogs—a group of about a dozen Golden Retrievers and yellow Labrador Retrievers who inspect new arrivals from behind a chain-link fence. With no food on offer, the dogs go back to lounging in the sun. Next to the front building is another large pen, this one filled with the paraphernalia of puppyhood: stuffed animals, tennis balls, and chew toys. A litter of six-month-old puppies sleep in a big pile of yellow fur.

Bonnie Bergin, founder and director of this revolutionary school, sits behind a desk in an office crowded with bookshelves, along with seven dogs. All seven get up to sniff a new visitor, wagging their tails and pushing their heads up to be patted, which stirs up quite a commotion in the small room.

"Ignore them and they'll settle down," Bonnie advises. It's hard to ignore all those pleading eyes and gentle pushes, but when you do, they go back to their spots and settle immediately. These dogs know the drill.

When they were young and newly married, Bonnie Bergin and her husband, Jim, were schoolteachers who wanted to see the world. They realized that teaching skills would be marketable around the globe, so they set off for Australia, where they got good jobs and saved up for more travel. They then visited the Philippines, Nepal, and India.

Bonnie was surprised at the number of people with disabilities on the streets of cities in Asia. She spoke about a man with no arms who sold newspapers on a busy street corner. A man who couldn't walk used his strong arms to pull himself up on his donkey to get around. Men on crutches offered flowers, magazines, or fruit for sale. Some sellers used their deformed feet like hands.

Bonnie and Jim were on their way home to the United States when they stopped off for a vacation tour of Turkey and found something irresistible about the place. They signed up for another year of teaching. After nine months, Jim's contract was up, but Bonnie stayed on, moving in with a friend. One evening, Bonnie and her friend lingered over dinner at a rooftop restaurant in Ankara.

"We were above a busy street, and when I looked down, I saw a man so disabled that he had to crawl on the ground like a snake," Bonnie remembers. "He was using his elbows to pull his entire body down the sidewalk. I was shocked. Then he got to the corner and pulled himself right across this six-lane freeway—right in the middle of Ankara. My mouth was hanging open. It's sort of the norm in Turkey, but it was one of the most shocking things I'd seen. He pulled himself out of sight. It was an amazing feat. This settled into the back of my mind. It was just something I filed away."

In pursuit of her interest in working with people with disabilities, Bonnie returned to Santa Rosa and enrolled in a master's degree program in special education at Sonoma State University. One day she tried to describe the experience of seeing so many people with disabilities in Asia. She was surprised when her teacher and fellow students didn't want to hear about it. They told her that Asia was a terrible place for people with disabilities. They contended that the American system of separating people with disabilities from society and keeping them where no one could see them was far more humane.

Bonnie decided to work on an idea that had come to her during her travels. She believed that people with disabilities would prefer to be out in the world. But unless they had a healthy person with them to push a wheelchair and open doors, they were stuck at home. She remembered how the disabled Chinese and Indians sold vegetables and fruits from their donkeys. Americans couldn't do that. But what animal that was widely accepted in American society could be used to help people with disabilities? Clearly, the answer was dogs. They were already widely used as guide dogs for the blind. This would be another step along that path.

"The people at school said, 'That's a terrible idea!' These students' mind-set was to institutionalize. I was thinking, 'How do you get people away from an institution and away from this kind of thinking? How do you change things so that people who are handicapped can have a life?'

"I had not realized how much I had learned from less-developed countries. When I got the idea of working with dogs, I thought: 'This is ideal. It will be like guide dogs.'"

Even though she was strongly discouraged from pursuing the idea, Bonnie thought to herself, "Why not?" The biggest problem, she figured, was her lack of experience with dogs. She had never trained a dog before and had no idea how to go about it. She knew she was an excellent teacher of children. She figured she'd use those skills.

The next hurdle was to find a person with a disability to work with. She was surprised when none of the people she contacted at homes for people with extreme disabilities or special-needs schools responded. In 1975, the idea of a person with a companion dog seemed ludicrous. Those first people she asked may have been afraid of being made fun of or being mistaken for being blind. But Bonnie didn't give up; she called the local senior center to see if there might be an elderly person there who would want to try her idea.

She explained what she had in mind to Kerry Knaus-Hardy,

the nineteen-year-old receptionist at the center. "Do you think anyone there would want to work with me?" Bonnie asked her, and Kerry answered, "I do."

Kerry had an unusual birth defect that left her with no use of her legs and very little mobility. "If her head fell to one side, she couldn't lift it back up—somebody had to do it for her," Bonnie recalled. Today Bonnie calls Kerry "the bravest person I ever met."

But Bonnie needed more than a collaborator. "I realized that I needed to know more about dogs, so I took a job at a kennel for two dollars an hour, picking up poop and feeding dogs. The guy I worked for was showing all different breeds at dog shows. I talked to some dog trainers and they said the same thing as the people in special education: 'No way. It won't work. You can't do it.' But I was so naïve that I really believed it could work."

In the service-dog industry, Bonnie Bergin is Christopher Columbus, Thomas Edison, the Wright Brothers. Using the same kind of original thinking that discovered America, invented the light bulb, or made man fly, she built on her idea step by step.

"I knew little about a dog's abilities," she says. "I tried to figure out everything that a dog could do for people with physical limits. I asked Kerry what she needed. She said, 'When I'm sitting in a room, and the attendant leaves, I end up sitting in the dark until they come back.' That was how we decided to teach dogs to turn light switches on and off.

"The irony is that, unbeknownst to me, at that time in the history of dog training, people were using very aversive methods—heavy choke chains and heavy handling. They were thinking of the dog as this animal that had to be really controlled, and how could somebody who doesn't have strength manage the dog? I loved dogs, but I had never learned a method of how to handle them."

The world's first service dog, Abdul, was the result of an

accidental breeding of Bonnie's Golden Retriever, Jada, and a neighbor's Labrador. "I used only positive techniques with Abdul. It was what I knew from teaching kids. And it worked. If it hadn't worked, I don't know what I'd be doing now."

Bonnie had found the perfect acolyte in Kerry, because she was dedicated and consistent. "Whatever I instructed her to do, she did. It was fantastic. Abdul was fantastic as well. He had two people who were just guessing about what he could do, but he paid attention and tried to learn what we wanted."

Bonnie and Kerry taught Abdul to pull a wheelchair, open doors, bring items from a table, pick up things Kerry dropped, pull a blanket across her, lie quietly at her side, accompany her whenever she left the house, retrieve her medicine from a counter, and go to get a human when she needed help. He could open the refrigerator and bring a bottle of water, retrieve keys and phones, even hand in credit cards at the grocery store and take back filled bags in return. Abdul learned many of the ninety commands that make up a service dog's repertoire today.

Seeing their success, a young disabled man in Kerry's neighborhood expressed interest in learning to work with a dog. Soon there was another person, and another. Pretty soon all of Bonnie's time was taken up teaching service, or assistance, dogs. The snowball had started to roll.

"Assistance dog" is a blanket term for any dog that provides a service for the disabled. This covers hearing dogs, who serve as ears for the deaf and hearing impaired; guide dogs, the eyes for those with visual impairments; and social/therapy dogs who improve the psychological or physical condition of children, adults, and the elderly.

"People kept telling me, you have to have an organization. Eventually I came up with a name and incorporated as Canine Companions for Independence. My sister sketched the logo."

So many people wanted a dog from CCI that the waiting list

kept growing and growing. The waiting list went from a year, to two years, to five and then ten years long.

"People were calling and asking me, 'Instead of waiting for so long to get a dog from you, can you teach me how to do it?' Back then, I didn't really like that idea. I thought to myself, 'If I do that, I'm building my own competition.' Instead, I set up regional bureaus of CCI. I was thinking like a CEO. I assumed that cornering the market was a good thing to do."

With hard work, long waiting lists, enthusiastic employees and volunteers, and eternally grateful clients, seventeen years went by. Bonnie had built a unique organization that was doing a lot of good in the world. But as she sorted through her bills and hired her staff, she was bothered by the thought that her very large organization was no longer truly flexible. Paperwork and scheduling and all sorts of administrative duties took up her time, when what she really wanted to do was pioneer even better methods of training dogs for the disabled. She shifted her priorities. Still the breakthrough thinker, she wondered how she could make it possible for more people to use service dogs. Instead of running a business that clearly was never going to be able to meet the huge demand, maybe it would be better to train others who could then go back to their own parts of the world and meet the demand there—a demand that Bonnie had in a sense created.

"I decided that I needed to be educating people about how to do it," she says. "I needed to spread the word about all the incredible things that dogs could do. And I couldn't do that at CCI."

After CCI, Bonnie built an umbrella nonprofit organization called Assistance Dogs International to help people anywhere who wanted to start a service dog program to get information about organizing such a service and training dogs for it. [Today there are more than 100 places in the United States where one can go to find a service dog. And these resources still can't meet the demand. See "Appendix: To Find Out More".]

What would be the best way to teach as many people as possible to train service dogs? The first idea Bonnie came up with was a summer seminar for dog trainers. There was great enthusiasm for the course. But real assistance-dog trainers need a lot more than that. Bonnie realized that what they needed was a college.

That led to the 1991 launch of the Assistance Dog Institute, a university-level school where students can get an Associate of Science, Bachelor of Science or Master of Science Degree in Assistance Dog Education. Later Bonnie added separate degrees in Human-Canine Life Sciences. With this education, the number of assistance dogs in society has grown exponentially. Bonnie has graduated students from all around the globe, including Japan, New Zealand, and Israel.

"I tell my students, you are here to learn what I learned. You take all that knowledge, and you leap from this point forward. You don't have to make all the mistakes I made again in order to get to where I am now. Uncover new and better things. Get that much more accomplished."

On the second floor of the institute, fifteen students in the Bachelor of Science program sit at desks with a lecturer at the top of their large circle. The students are listening to ethics professor Deni Elliott teach "Ethical, Moral, and Legal Perspectives of Canine Training, Use, and Ownership." It's a standard university setting, except that each student has a golden or yellow dog snoozing at his or her feet. The dogs lift their eyelids when a stranger tiptoes into class to observe. These dogs are learning the important lesson that they must follow their owner/leader everywhere, getting up only on the human's schedule, not their own.

One of the problems Bonnie Bergin faced in the early years of her career was the difficulty in figuring out which dogs would be good assistance dogs and which would not make it. Dogs donated and accepted into the training program had a very low rate of success. CCI was breeding dogs, but even among those, after a year's work and thousands of dollars invested, only 25 percent would graduate to the work they were trained for. The others would have to be placed into pet homes.

That was not enough—a lot of effort was being wasted. When she realized she could probably do something about this problem, Bonnie says, "I went from suits, power lunches, and a lucrative salary to shoveling poop in literally days." She was searching for a way of quantifying what a service dog was and how to breed one.

She studied all the available material on dog breeding. The Inuit breed the strongest and fastest sled dogs to one another; racetracks breed the swiftest greyhound to another winning racer; hunters breed their best male bird-pointer to their best female bird-hunter. In each case, strength in a particular characteristic is created. Bonnie studied Belyaev's research on the "friendly foxes," discovering that when he created a more domesticated fox, physical traits followed, such as softer, silkier coats and dropped ears. She realized that a line of dogs whose instincts and trainability were ideally suited for this work would also most likely have similar physical traits.

When you look around the Assistance Dog Institute, you see the cream of this genetic crop—dogs whose abilities start with a dose of the right genes. One of the first things an astute observer will notice is that all of these dogs are blonds. In Labrador Retriever kennels you normally see yellow, black, and chocolate Labs. Here, the color is confined to yellows. Where are the black Labrador Retrievers?

There are none, and it has nothing to do with personal preference for one color over another. It has to do with Bonnie's theory about neoteny, the retention of childlike traits in an adult animal.

Bonnie compiled a list of the characteristics she was looking for. "We have to have an unobtrusive helpmate, because people with disabilities can't manage an overactive dog. If they are spending all their time telling the dog, 'No!' and dealing with an unruly animal, it's not serving them. So 'unobtrusive' is one of the guidelines."

She clicks off a list of other qualities: the dog can't take too much initiative; the dog can't be too predatory; the dog can't be "high arousal."

"We are looking for a service dog that doesn't have those characteristics. Who wouldn't have those characteristics in a human? A child—a very young child, about five years old, generally does what Mommy says, helps Mommy with the dishes, and bonds strongly with the parents. Rather than questioning the parents, they are compliant.

"When they get older, they get independent. What's the role of a teenager? To pull away from Mom and establish his or her own independence. We don't want a service dog who is pulling away from its human partner and trying to establish independence."

This, Bonnie pointed out, is why she decided to work with Goldens and Labs. But which Golden and Labs? How could you tell which ones were going to pass the course, and which ones would not?

The Golden Retriever standard calls for "rich, lustrous golden of various shades." Yellow Labrador Retrievers should "range in color from fox-red to light cream." At ADI, the dogs are only the very lightest shades, almost white. Dogs of these colors, Bonnie found, retain their neotenized, or childlike, traits, while the darker colors develop more independence.

"Think about a baby; a human child often has lighter hair and lighter skin. The lighter-colored dogs turned out to be more childlike. This is not 100-percent reliable. This is not something you could take to the bank. But for us, it's a guideline."

Ears had another trait that went along with neoteny. "My theory is that the more cartilage there is in the ear, the less juvenile the dog." She points out differences among the seven dogs in her office. Dogs with thicker cartilage whose ears rise up when they are interested in a sound or movement; dogs with less cartilage have ears that flop loosely by the side of the head.

"We look for ears that aren't 'up.' One of the things we're having a problem with is that the ears are not being lifted up off the ear canal. When you have the ear flat on the ear canal, with no air going in and out, you get ear problems. Well, I would much prefer that the person with the disability, or his or her attendant, have to squirt a little powder in the ears now and then rather than have a dog that might pull him or her down the street and out into traffic."

A little ear trouble turned out to be part of the solution.

Bonnie did a lot of research with many breeds before settling on the Golden, Labrador, and Golden Lab crosses. "What is your image of a German Shepherd? A dog that is protective and can think on its own," she reasons. "A German Shepherd is not child-like. It doesn't say, 'Mommy, Mommy, what do you want me to do?' It says, 'Something has to be done and I'm going to do it, unless you are powerful enough to stop me.' "Their place is with the police. That's a good place for a German Shepherd.

"I'm exaggerating for effect here," she concedes. But for the most part, the average German Shepherd would not be appropriate. The average Belgian Malinois would not be appropriate. But how many policemen do you see being protected by a Golden Retriever?

"So we're looking at Goldens and Labs as the soft 'Mommy' dog. And in that continuum of Goldens and Labs, we don't want the field trial ones. We want them to have less initiative than that. We want them to be less aroused than that. We want them to look at Mommy and say, 'What can I do?'"

Next physical trait—the tail. "The tail of any animal, and certainly any dog, goes up and down with arousal," Bonnie says. "On the lower-aroused dogs, the tail just hangs. The higher-aroused dogs, the tails are much higher. We need low arousal. So we look for a dog with a lower tail carriage."

Lower-tail carriage was fashionable in retrievers for a time, and during those years, Bonnie found acceptable dogs she could acquire. But the fad changed and tail carriage went back up. Lately, there are almost no retrievers being bred by kennels that can make the grade.

So Bonnie went to Europe. "I figured, here's a place where there are no rules against dogs. Dogs go everywhere, into stores, restaurants, trains, everywhere that people go. So it must be that they are breeding a dog who knows how to fit in those environments. Which means that at least when we get a Lab from Europe, it is easygoing, doesn't fight, is comfortable going in and out of stores." Her hunch turned out to be true. Two Golden Retrievers came back from England with Bonnie, and another two from France, and then two from Austria.

Only seven years after she began her breeding program, ADI's dogs achieved an 80-percent success rate, a remarkable feat in such a short space of time. Eight out of ten of the dogs Bonnie bred could complete the training course and graduate to a placement.

Bonnie says that she was amazed at the dogs' intelligence and proficiency. They seemed to be able to learn everything she asked of them. She started wondering: *What if they could read?*

For a person with a handicap, it could be useful to tell the dog, "Exit," and have the dog look for and locate the appropriate sign, then go there. The same would be true for "Restroom" or "Park." A sniffer dog could communicate better if he learned to point to a card that named the scent he had picked up—"Gun" or "Meat" or "Cocaine." And a reading dog would be an incredible motivator of children who were reluctant to learn to read.

So Bonnie wrote the words "Sit," "Down," and "Stay" on big

sheets of paper, and set out to teach her own dogs, Lexus and Keila, to read.

"It was straight classical conditioning," Bonnie says. She showed Keila the "Down" card, asked her to lie down, and gave her a reward. Within one lesson, whenever she showed the word, Keila lay down. Lesson learned. Keila could read.

Using that method, she got the two dogs up to a 20-word vocabulary. An unanticipated thing started to happen. The dogs started to learn new things even better than they had before. They seemed to be able to conceptualize and problem-solve, traits that would make them of even greater use when placed with a person with a disability. Bonnie learned that the ability to read required coordination from four parts of the brain, making it a very advanced cognitive task.

"Then when I was doing my research one summer, I realized that humans had begun communicating in the earliest years with stick figures. Then they turned stick figures sideways because there were only so many stick figures that people could remember, and that's how they invented writing.

"Also, in China and Japan I found that the dogs they were training there could differentiate the Chinese and Japanese characters, with all the slashes. You wouldn't think they could, because dogs don't have refined vision, but the cards were just held up and they would read them."

She started showing her dogs stick figures, and they responded. Again, it was simple classical conditioning. It didn't seem very exciting. But then came an accident that rocked her world.

"We were at a big convention, and we were supposed to do a demonstration of how we teach the dogs. One of the trainers, Jorjan, had a dog that could read the cards but had never seen the stick figures. So I told her, 'Go up onstage with these two stick figure cards and teach Norton what to do.'

"But Jorjan didn't hear me. So when she went up onstage,

she didn't go through the procedure of teaching the dog. She just held up the card. I was sitting in the back of the auditorium, thinking, 'Oh, no, Jorjan, you've messed it up—you're supposed to teach the dog!' The dog stood there, studying the card with the stick figure of a dog sitting, really concentrating on it. I felt so embarrassed for him. And then suddenly—the dog sat."

Bonnie's jaw dropped. "I thought, '*This can't be happening—she has to teach him first.*' Then she showed him the other card, the one with the dog lying down. He studied it. And he did it! He lay down.

"All I could think was, this is not possible! It amazed me. I saw how I had underestimated our dogs all this time. I was going slow, teaching one thing at a time. And this dog had made a gigantic leap in cognition, and I didn't even know that he was capable of it. I thought, Good lord, what else can these dogs do that we haven't thought to ask them about?"

Through experiments back home, Bonnie discovered that a dog could only interpret a stick figure if he had already been taught to read words. He had to know the basic step that when he looked at a card, he was supposed to do something. "The fact that they can look at something that is symbolic and assign meaning to it is phenomenal."

She tried an experiment with four different dogs who had already been taught reading. At different locations and at different times, so the dogs couldn't learn from each other, she held up a stick figure of a dog lifting his paw to "Shake."

"They'd never done 'shake'—they didn't know that command," Bonnie recalls. So they didn't offer to shake. The dogs looked at the card, didn't know what it meant, and started to offer behaviors from their repertoire: roll, sit, lay down. They'd look at us, like, what is it you want from me? And we didn't tell them. The first dog got tired of offering us every behavior she could think of. She got up and came over to the card and looked and looked and looked. And then she did this…." Bonnie raises her hand slightly. The dog was mimicking what she saw on the card. She lifted her paw.

And it wasn't just one dog. After several sessions, all four of the dogs lifted their paws.

"The more I do this work, the more I am amazed at their ability. We haven't come close to figuring out what they can do. Exploring that canine mind further is what really excites me."

After hearing about an experiment in England in which dogs were taught to recognize the smell of cancer cells, Bonnie put that next on her list. But while talking to a vintner at her husband's barbecue restaurant, she realized that dogs could be of tremendous help in Sonoma Valley's big industry, winemaking.

The vineyard owners were suffering tremendous losses because of a pest called the "vine mealybug," a small, sap-sucking insect that is coated with a white, powdery wax that resembles meal. A few individual insect scouts will move in on the roots of a vine and then send for their entire family. Quickly, a large colony forms and kills the vine, then spreads to its neighbor. The mealybug is a serious pest, because winemakers don't want to spray their vines with toxic chemicals to kill it. There is no known natural preventative, except to discover those first few scouts and get them out before the mealybugs launch a takeover. The problem is that they are tiny and humans can't see them—not until the colony has grown large and damaging. Bonnie recognized both a challenge and an earning opportunity. If her dogs could sniff out the mealybugs and save the vineyards, maybe the vintners would pay for the service. It would be a way to bring some badly needed funds into the institute.

Bonnie had no doubt that her dogs could learn to recognize the mealybug scent. "We took a new litter of puppies and started mixing the scent in their food, so that scent would become very important to them."

The hard part would be to teach the dogs that when they

found that scent, they should alert the handler. At first, Bonnie taught the dogs to sit when they found an infected vine and wait until the handler came up. But the vintners didn't like that behavior. They wanted a dog who would work up and down the rows of vines alone, and when it found the scent, bark.

Bonnie laughs when she remembers what happened next. "Here were our wonderful service dogs, whom we call Velcro dogs because they never want to leave our sides. They were so slow! They didn't want to take the initiative to go down the rows of vines. They wanted the handlers to be with them all the time."

Back to the breeding room. She needed a dog with more independence and a higher level of arousal. It took just a year to breed animals who were better at patrolling the vineyards.

"We took one of our higher-aroused females and brought in an outside male. And the difference was like night and day. You watch these dogs go out there, and their heads are up and excited. You can't hold them back, they are so anxious to go do the work. To our service dogs, this is not exciting. The vineyard people said they wanted the dog to go there and bark—so we taught that."

Bonnie points out that when she first started training service dogs, everyone told her it couldn't be done. Back then, she says, "I was not looking at dogs as though they were these amazing animals with incredible minds." She just figured they could handle some simple physical tasks that could help the disabled.

As a teacher, she began to notice, through newspapers reports and from her own friends, something that disturbed her very much. The new generation of high school students seemed adrift in a sea of meaningless activities. She'd spent years teaching high school and still loved the excitement of seeing students expand and grow as they reached out in their universe. Now, she heard of so many who dropped out, turned to crime, were involved in violent fights, and became addicted to drugs. They seemed to have no sense of purpose. They were not developing a good sense of personal responsibility.

What could be better, she mused, than having a dog in their lives? A dog provided those things. Her program for High Risk High School Teens was born.

In Bonnie Bergin's conception of the universe, there is no end to the kinds of tasks that dogs can do.

CHAPTER 9

BIG DOG IN TROUBLED PLACES

WHILE BONNIE BERGIN was in Sonoma County dreaming up the beginnings of a program for at-risk teens, Rick Yount, a sandy-haired, easygoing social worker was wrestling with his Golden Retriever, Gabe, who was trying to prevent him from going out the door and off to work. Gabe had been a wonderful and welcome Christmas present from good friends, and he was growing into a happy and loving companion. But he hated one thing: being left alone all day. He was trying as hard as he could to convince Rick that if he stayed home alone one more day, he would perish.

Now it was running late, and Rick's mind was on the day ahead. He didn't have time to play with Gabe anymore; he told him curtly, "Okay, okay," and let Gabe climb into the back of his Toyota for the drive to work. Gabe was overjoyed. Rick told him he might not like it as much once he'd sat in the car for eight hours in the parking lot until quitting time.

Rick's job involved working with abused and neglected children. Today's task was particularly heartbreaking; he had to remove an eleven-year-old boy from his birth mother's home because of abuse and neglect.

"The kid didn't want to go. He fought us. We were villains, taking him away from the only home he had ever known," Rick said. "The poor kid was sobbing in the back of my car. He wouldn't communicate with us at all.

"A mile or two down the road, all of a sudden, the sobbing stopped. I looked in my rearview mirror. I thought: 'What happened? Did the kid jump out of the car?' But what I saw was the head of a Golden Retriever lying in the boy's lap. That was Gabe, trying to comfort him. The boy was petting him and stroking him, and it was obvious the kid felt much better. Like he had a friend."

One of Rick's co-workers was with him and saw the transformation. One minute, the kid's heart was breaking, the next, he was okay. She kept talking about it to everyone back at the office. Gabe came to work the next day, and the next. When Rick went to visit children in foster care or transitional living situations, Gabe went with him. These children had been either beaten or abandoned by their birth parents. They faced tough, stressful, emotionally jarring lives, many with no parent or relative to hug and console them. With Gabe there, they had a loving presence who was only interested in giving out kisses.

Pretty soon, Gabe didn't have to stay out in the parking lot. He was a welcome guest. The social workers joked that Gabe was the best worker in the department. And he didn't get paid. When Rick took him on visits to schools, the kids would gather around and pet him in groups. He loved it, and they loved it.

"There was one case—I had a little girl named Gina who was

a victim of sexual abuse. I had to remove her from one home and put her into another home, right in the middle of her kindergarten year. Besides having had all this trauma, she was expected to readjust to a new kindergarten class. She was very timid about going in and making new friends. She asked if Gabe could go to school with her."

Rick took her on the first day of school. She entered the classroom holding Gabe's leash. The other kids were impressed. She let go of Gabe's leash and he went up and down each row, stopping at each desk to say hello. He paid attention to each kid in the room. Rick watched him, amazed. Gabe had instinctively known what to do to break the ice. Instead of a role as the geeky new kid, Gina was the kid who brought the "cool" dog.

Rick kept track of her over the years. "She's a teenager now. She was one of our success stories. We got her the placement she needed; she was adopted with her three siblings. She's in a good home."

On the Web site of the West Virginia adoption network, the kids' first names and a small bio of each was posted. There was Gina's new family, sitting there on the steps with Gabe. One small boy was a little devil; he's holding his fingers in rabbit ears above Gabe's head.

In another case, a nine-year-old boy, Jake, who had been in foster homes for three years, was being put up for adoption. His foster parents were providing a good, stable home, but adoption was just not part of their plans. Rick would have liked to leave him there, since he was content. But a state order came down to get him into an adoptive home.

Another worker arranged for Jake to meet a couple who were eager to adopt. They had the couple show up at his school, brought him out of class and put them all in a room together. Things were not going well. Little Jake was scared to death. He hid behind his book bag and wouldn't talk to them.

"The case manager called me and asked me to bring Gabe to his office. I found this odd, because he was a person who didn't usually think much of Gabe's abilities. Yet we were close to the school so I took Gabe right over.

"Gabe knew the job really well by this time. He had his own way of doing things. He usually went right up to the kid because he knew the child needed reassurance. This time, we went in, and the kid perked up, looking at Gabe, but Gabe did not run over to him. He stopped, and then went to the couple, which was very different from what he usually did. I was going to call him and urge him to go to the kid, but I thought, 'See what happens.'

"The prospective parents fell all over Gabe. They started petting him and talking to him. They were so stressed out over this meeting that petting a dog really relaxed them. They talked to Gabe, telling him he's a good boy, a beautiful, wonderful dog, smart, handsome, all kinds of nice things. Instead of being so tense, they started acting like normal people.

"The kid just watched them from behind his book bag. He was listening to how the couple treated Gabe. He could see they were nice people.

"Then Gabe went over to him. Gabe reached up and put his paw on the book bag. The kid peeked out at him and Gabe wagged his tail. It was like he was saying, 'I checked them out for you, buddy.'

"The kid still didn't want to talk. Of course, Gabe is a Golden Retriever, he loves to play ball. He dreams about playing ball. So I went out to the car and got a ball and gave it to the couple. They threw it, and Gabe brought it back. So the couple rolled the ball, and then it 'accidentally' rolled over and bumped the kid's leg. So he leaned down and rolled it back. That broke his resistance. Once he moved, he wanted to get in the game. Pretty soon, we had a game of catch going in the room, involving everybody.

"Gabe used himself as a segue between the couple and the kid. It's uncanny how he knew how to do that."

The social worker's plan now called for the boy to go out to lunch with the couple. Jake indicated this was out of the question. Under no circumstances would he go anywhere with people he didn't know. He wanted to stay at school, which was the only stable place he knew.

Rick saw what was going on and said: "Hey, I heard you are going to a pizza place for lunch. Listen, would you do me a favor? Gabe's favorite food in the world is pizza crust, and he hasn't had any in a long time. I told him he would get some soon. Would you mind bringing back some pizza crust for him?

"The kid thinks about it. He was still resistant. I said, 'Listen, if you go out and get that pizza crust, when you get back I'll give you a ride in my car with Gabe to take you home.'

"The kid said that he was okay with that. It still amazes me to this day how Gabe handled that. He's a better social worker than I am."

Rick investigated the various therapy-dog programs and got Gabe certification with Therapy Dogs Incorporated, based in Cheyenne, Wyoming.

Gabe's career had started by happenstance. But every day there was a role at Rick's agency that a dog could play. He could reach kids who were hard to reach. Rick took him on emergencies, when children had to be moved from dangerous situations, often where abuse was involved. He took him when he went to check on children who had been moved to foster homes. A psychologist working for the state heard about Gabe, and asked Rick to let Gabe stay for a counseling session with an eight-year-old girl who'd undergone sexual abuse. Psychologists find it difficult to evaluate abuse victims because the abused will do anything to avoid talking about what happened, even throw books and open desk drawers and scream at people outside the window.

But this time, the girl settled down with her arms around Gabe. She answered questions into Gabe's neck, which was fine because the psychologist was able to get a lot of information. Gabe was a comforting and reassuring presence. He made the session much easier.

When the girl had to appear in family court, Rick and Gabe picked her up and Gabe walked with her, up the steps of the courthouse and down a long hall. They sat together in a back room. The eight-year-old was so frightened she shook. She could hardly stand up. She was clutching Gabe, practically choking him, but he didn't object. It was as if he were telling her he was strong enough to hold her up through this ordeal.

"These court hearings are gruesome," Rick says. "The kids have to tell about horrible sexual abuse they've been through at the hands of their birth parents. They don't want to talk about that. The defense attorneys grill them and try to get the kids rattled. It's awful. Gabe couldn't go in to court when she testified, but I had him waiting outside the door for when she came out."

Gabe's fame spread after the court hearing. Psychologists wanted him at intake sessions with kids; prosecutors wanted him comforting the victims when they were brought to court. For someone who didn't speak English, Gabe was playing a big role in making things run smoothly.

As word of Gabe's work spread throughout the county, Gabe was named United Way Volunteer of the Month and represented the United Way at parades and ceremonies. His picture was in the paper, meeting with the governor.

One evening, Rick's mother called from Pittsburgh to ask if he'd seen the news magazine program *20/20*. A segment was shown about a woman named Bonnie Bergin in California, who got high school students to raise and train assistance dogs to work with handicapped people.

"When I saw that tape, I said 'Wow, I'm doing that.' The kids were training the dogs using the exact same skill set I was trying to teach teens who had never had any parenting. It was the same skill set I was trying to get foster parents to use. You need an experiential way of teaching parenting skills. You can't pick those up from reading a book. No one is going to let teens go into a daycare center and practice on human babies. We were giving teens preprogrammed little dolls to work with, but they weren't alive, so there was no bonding and no shaping of behaviors.

"When I saw that video, I went crazy. I convinced the agency I worked for that the best thing in the world they could do was to send me out to go through the training."

That's exactly what happened; he signed up for the Assistance Dog Institute's intensive summer course. Rick says, "I went out and soaked up as much as I could."

In Bonnie Bergin, Rick found a teacher, mentor, and kindred spirit. He returned from the summer enthusiastic about expanding the roles dogs could play in healing and helping their human friends. With Gabe, he had taught himself how to use the soothing, calming, stabilizing effect of a dog's presence. Bonnie's ideas opened up many more avenues. Rick got a grant to start the Golden Rule Assistance Dog Program, the first program of its kind in West Virginia. Rick and volunteers from the psychology department of the University of West Virginia traveled four days a week to the Morgan Alternative Learning Center, a school for at-risk teens, taking with them seven Golden Retrievers.

He says the kids were fascinated by the dogs and eager to help in their training. They started when the dogs were puppies, and they all trained for two years in order to teach them all the aspects of caring for a person with a handicap, including learning the ninety basic service dog commands.

What worked so well about the program, Rick says, is that it provided a way to get through to the kids the importance of patience, kindness, and praise, while also teaching them parenting skills without lecturing them about those things.

"The kids had to learn how to set limits without losing your cool," Rick says. "They saw how a bad mood in parent could affect a child. Dogs are just like kids. If you get frustrated and angry with them, they shut down. When you're teaching a dog, you have to sound stern like Arnold Schwarzenegger and then switch to praising like Richard Simmons in less than two-tenths of a second. That's emotion regulation. It's hard for these kids to learn. They could learn it in this setting because it wasn't about them."

Rick eventually realized that teaching teens to train service dogs for other people was what he really liked to do best. The best place to do that was the Assistance Dog Institute. Soon he was on ADI's permanent staff, living in California, where, he said, "there were more people out on the road here every day than the entire population of West Virginia."

He continues the work that Bonnie had begun with at-risk teens in the Santa Rosa–area high schools.

CHAPTER 10

MY PUPPY, YOUR INDEPENDENCE

THE UPSTAIRS BALLROOM of the Crest Hollow Country Club has thick, colorful carpets and a five-tiered chandelier with hundreds of shiny crystals. Sparkling light is reflected in the full-length mirrors that line the walls. It's a place where young couples in love swoon at their wedding receptions and executives from companies with budgets the size of Argentina toast one another with Cristal champagne.

But on a March Saturday afternoon, several hundred people took seats to applaud the graduates of one of the most selective schools in the world. There are so many applicants for so few openings at this school that it is harder to get into than Harvard or Yale or Princeton. It was the graduation ceremony for seven, just seven, people with handicaps who had been selected to receive service dogs from Canine Companions for Independence.

From now on, their difficult lives would be shared with seven very special dogs. For the past two weeks, the dogs and humans had been in training so that the new owners could become familiar with the signals and commands the dogs knew, and the dogs could be trained to any specific tasks the owner needed. The dogs had an extensive repertoire. They could retrieve dropped wallets, push elevator buttons, help with the laundry, bring the telephone, get beverages from the refrigerator, open the door, pick up a pencil, or give assistance in getting up from a chair. They could turn lights off and on, open doors, pull wheelchairs, bark to alert other humans that their partner needed help, brace to give their partner support, open and close cupboards, and bring medication. They could hand cash to cashiers and bring back change in return. They could bring clothing and shoes to help their partner get dressed. They could undo Velcro ankle braces. They could pick up a penny or a crutch. Their new partners would no longer be stranded at the front door because they'd dropped their keys. No telephone would be out of their reach. Some service dogs could even summon an ambulance using a specially adapted phone they could step on to call for help.

These dogs were amazing.

All those tasks are usually done every day for a person with a handicap by family members or a nurse or a hired caretaker. Those are tasks that keep wheelchair-bound people locked alone in a room, unable to do anything but wait for someone to help them. What these dogs represented to these seven people was something most people take for granted—physical mobility. The potential to get along on their own for a few hours or perhaps even a whole day. Freedom.

The other quality the dogs brought to their partners was something more emotional. Like dogs the world over, they would sit lovingly next to their human companions and comfort them when they were feeling down. They would provide a shoulder to lean on during times of frustration. They would be friends to people whose physical limitations kept them from making many friends.

A young girl in a wheelchair told me: "When Oscar is with me, people don't stare at me. They're looking at him. He makes everybody smile."

People with service dogs reported time after time that one of the biggest benefits that came with their dog was the public's willingness to speak to them. It turns out that people in wheelchairs are aware of the stares they attract and feel uncomfortable about being so obviously different. But studies confirmed that when they have a dog with them, members of the public are ten times more likely to smile and say hello. They don't feel like a person with a disability; they are a person with a dog, just like anybody else. The dog is a great leveler. In other words, having a dog there causes human beings to treat people with disabilities like fellow human beings.

The bill for a service dog until he reaches about eighteen months or two years includes vet bills, food, board, kennel help, special equipment, and a trainer who works with the dog almost every day. The people at CCI figure it comes to about $45,000. That's about what it costs to attend Harvard University for a year, when you consider tuition and housing. You can get a government subsidized tuition loan to pay for your Harvard education. At Canine Companions for Independence, acquiring a service dog is free. The organization pays the bills totally through private donations.

CCI trains four types of assistance dogs, which they call Canine Companions. There are "service dogs" for adults with physical disabilities; "hearing dogs" for those who are deaf or hard of hearing; "facility dogs," who work permanently in a health care setting, and "skilled companions," a designation they use for dogs going to children or adults who have developmental or cognitive disabilities along with their physical disabilities, such that they can't manage the dog on their own and need the help of another human. In these cases, the dog, the person with a disability, and human assistant are trained together as a team.

A CCI booklet at the graduation proclaimed, "The most advanced technology to transform the lives of people with disabilities has a cold nose and a warm heart."

The regional president of CCI took the podium first. "We are quite a family," he said. He joked that he wanted to align his solidarity with black Labs because there had been complaints lately that black Labs get no respect. Golden Retrievers and yellow LGXs (shorthand for Labrador-Golden crosses) were starting to make up a larger percentage of the dogs in service. They were getting all the attention. Some people seemed to think he was favoring yellow dogs over black ones, he said, but he liked both colors equally. He raised an arm encircled by a black band to show his support. This is an inside joke at CCI, and the crowd laughed delightedly. The black-versus-yellow color controversy has diehard supporters on both sides of the argument. Making everyone laugh about it was a good way to remind everybody that first and foremost and in spite of color, they are all wonderful dogs.

He thanked the many helpers and trainers, the interviewer who screens thousands of people who are desperate to be in the program, the interns, the fundraisers, and the facilities manager. Then he welcomed the group that made up the majority of the people sitting in the seats, most of them with a young dog at their side, the Puppy Raisers.

In CCI circles, Puppy Raisers are held in high esteem. These people volunteer to accept a wiggling eight-week-old puppy into their homes; feed, exercise, groom, socialize, and care for him for 16 months; pay vet bills that include spaying or neutering; and teach him forty commands. They put up with housetraining accidents, chewed shoes, and scratched doors; teach him to sit and shake and lie down; cart him to family vacations and picnics in the park; accustom him to strangers, cars, children, hospitals, joggers, cats, noisy streets, and then, when all their work has produced a solid, well-socialized, obedient member of their own family, give him back. It is a sacrifice of monumental proportions.

A Puppy Raiser from Virginia spoke about the love they have for these dogs. "We give dogs the space we can spare. They give us their all. While they're with us, they provide solace and calm for our own children." His voice wavered a little as he said, "Tonight, about 80 percent of our emotions are running down the leash. But 100 percent of their emotions are coming back up it."

A high school student named Wendi Hartman took the stage with a Golden Retriever at her side to talk about what it was like to be a Puppy Raiser. The dog dropped nonchalantly to the floor when she began to speak. This was Reege, her third puppy as signment from CCI. When she'd started with her first puppy, she said, she was twelve years old. She spoke about being a shy and reclusive child. Charged with the responsibility to raise a confident puppy, she realized she would have to change. She could not be standoffish and aloof anymore, because the puppy needed a confident leader.

"I was usually too scared to look people in the eyes," Wendi said about her personality before she had that first puppy. "But I forced myself to learn. I had to."

She discovered that with that first black Labrador Retriever at her side, "People chase you down grocery store aisles to tell you, 'He reminds me of my grandmother's boyfriend's daughter's dog, who died ten years ago, except that he was small and blond and fluffy and had blue eyes—compared to my Lab, who was big and black and smooth haired and had dark-eyes. But otherwise, he looks just like him.'"

Laughs of recognition ripped through the audience. Wendi said she always stopped to acknowledge such people and let them pat the dog on the head. "It's silly, but you realize you made their day a little better with just this little encounter."

With the CCI puppy by her side, Wendi learned to be brave, like the Cowardly Lion from *The Wizard of Oz*. The Cowardly Lion thought he had no courage, until he roared to life to defend Dorothy, someone he loved. Wendi Hartman discovered she didn't need a Badge of Courage to get her puppy out in public to meet people. Like the Cowardly Lion, she was equipped with inner courage, too.

The people at CCI had prepared a video of the seven canine graduates. Uncoordinated little puppies romped across lawns and sat quietly in kitchens at the homes of their Puppy Raisers. Several months later, they were galloping teenagers, chasing tennis balls and heeling through shopping malls. The last shots showed each puppy, now grown and trained, at CCI, sitting at attention by the side of their new partner, about to embark on a life of service. The lyrics of the Beatles's song, "All You Need Is Love," were followed by the equally heartbreaking song, "You'll Be in My Heart." My impression was that the Puppy Raisers bore up stoically through this touching video, but I'm not sure because I couldn't see very well at that point. The tears streaming from my eyes got in the way.

The father of a child who was getting a Skilled Companion said that until these two weeks of training, they had not realized how much the Puppy Raisers had contributed toward creating a useful service dog.

"They work with unimaginable dedication," he said. "We would not be here today if it was not for the decision they made to put a year's worth of effort into raising and training these puppies—and then willingly giving the puppy back to be an assistant to someone else.

"Someone very smart said, 'You owe it to your dog to be worthy of such devotion.' Well, we're going to try to be, for the rest of our lives."

One of the ways that CCI takes care of its Puppy Raisers is by inviting them to this ceremony. They have not seen their puppy since he bounced out of their lives a year ago. He has grown into a mature dog, calmer, thoroughly trained and dedicated to his new work.

The seven human graduates came up on stage, each one carrying a single rose. The first was a young man in a wheelchair, Mark Baker of Vermont. He was getting his second service dog, after spending eight years with his first one.

Wendi Hartman led Reege, the black Lab she had raised, onto the stage, and formally handed over the leash to Mark. He handed her the single yellow rose. Their hands touched. Wendi smiled at Reege with a look that was almost wistful. Reege was looking at Mark to see what he wanted to do next.

Then came Ayla Caldwell, a young girl who said her favorite activity was watching Animal Planet. She patted the blond head of her new dog, Landon, already at his position next to her wheelchair. She said after two weeks of training, he was already her best buddy.

Young Jonathan Moor had desperately wanted a service dog, but understood that his chances of getting one were slim. When the letter of acceptance arrived in the month of December, his parents wrapped it in a big box and gave it to him for Christmas.

"That was the best Christmas he ever had," said his father. Jonathan was going home with Morse, a yellow Lab. Morse would be part of the team that included Jonathan's parents.

A musician, Vince Norman, came from upstate New York, where he had his own music production company. Puppy Raisers Jennifer and John Schmidt, in matching brown shirts, presented him with Gedrick, a black Lab. Gedrick reared up to put his big black paws on Vince's lap, then looked out at the audience in delight when they applauded him.

Vince said that in the two short weeks he'd known Gedrick, they experienced an intense bonding. He said he found his experience with CCI "inspiring on every level."

Seventh-grader Maddie Paolero had pale brown hair and an angelic smile. Her mom, Beth, wheeled her forward as she was introduced as a girl who sings in the choir at church and is sometimes a spokesmodel for the Muscular Dystrophy Foundation. When the black Lab, Reno, was presented to her, he snuffled up to her face and covered her cheeks with kisses while she laughed.

Brittany Borgen was watched over by her mother, Lisa. Now, a yellow Lab named Lok would share the duty. Her mother was obviously grateful for any kind of physical or mental progress with Brittany. Lok had already had a positive effect because when he was around, Brittany was motivated to reach for him and hug him, which got her to coordinate her uncooperative muscles. Lok didn't seem to think the job was very hard. As the announcer spoke, he stretched and wagged his tail.

The final graduating team was TJ Brown from New York, an autistic first grader being presented with a yellow Lab, Kermit. When he walked onstage with his mother, he unwittingly gave the audience a taste of what life with an autistic child is like. First he put his arms up over his head and fell flat to the floor. With incredible patience, his mother, Nancy Herard, tried to get him to stand up, but it's impossible to force a child to maintain a standing position, so he slumped back down each time. The Puppy Raiser tried to hand Kermit's leash to TJ, but he ignored her and ran off the stage at full speed. Nancy accepted the dog, trying in vain to summon TJ to come back. He made a mad dash for the stage platform, raced across it and ran at full speed off the other side. As the Puppy Raiser accepted a rose from Nancy, TJ ran by the group, still at full speed, not even stopping to look at the dog.

The graduates gathered onstage to sing a song they had written called "The Doggie Bunch." Some of the lines were,

> Our dogs are trained by angels here on earth.
> We won't let them expand in girth.

When the ceremony was over, the crowd mingled into groups of three or four, the Puppy Raisers sending their best wishes to the new partners. Many had young dogs with them because they were raising another puppy for CCI, and a graduation ceremony is just the sort of setting they look for to accustom the puppy to crowds and noises.

Some were there for "Turn In," the act of giving back the dog they had raised for the past year. The Puppy Raisers are a strong bunch. They were mostly able to keep their eyes clear as they turned their charges over to the CCI staff, and most of the dogs walked out of their lives without looking back. It seemed a little sad that the puppy would not fight to get back to the family that had raised him, but one of the Puppy Raisers told me it's not sad at all, it's an accomplishment. "If your puppy walks out that door without even a backward glance at you, it means you have raised him to be confident and trusting. That's the kind of confidence he needs."

Each person hoped and prayed that the puppy they had raised would be walking out of this ballroom next year as a graduate. The dogs who don't meet the demanding requirements of working with the handicapped are released; sometimes going back to the Puppy Raiser as a pet, but often moving on to another job at police or military or medical organizations. These dogs continue to serve by using their confidence, ultra-sensitive noses and willingness to please, functioning as bomb searchers, border patrol, customs inspectors, and therapy dogs.

The average service life of a dog is eight years. After that he is retired and lives out his golden years as a pet.

Some of the Puppy Raisers were heading over to CCI headquarters on their way out, where they would pick up a new puppy.

CCI graduated 178 teams in 2006. It has 1,237 active graduates. 2,562 teams have been put in place since Bonnie Bergin founded CCI in 1975.

CCI is trying to bring service dogs to every person who needs one. Its mission is awe-inspiring. The devotion of its members is palpable. The organization has five regional centers and two satellite offices, and it obviously needs a lot more. Nationwide, CCI counts 623 Puppy Raisers, 95 Breeder Caretakers, and more than 3,000 volunteers. The Lions Club has been a major source of donations, volunteers, and publicity for the organization.

One of the Puppy Raisers was smiling gently as she watched the graduates exit with their dogs on their way to their new lives. "Aren't you sad about turning in your puppy?" I asked her.

"You have memories you'll never lose," she said.

She reminded me of something the high school Puppy Raiser, Wendi, had said. "I went to CCI expecting to make an impact on someone else's life. I never expected such an impact in my own life."

The people who work with CCI are trying to provide a person who is handicapped with a "service dog," a permanent canine partner who will make the handicap a little easier to bear. Not everyone can do this work. Not everyone can become so close to an animal they will one day have to surrender. There are other jobs for canines who are first and foremost beloved pets, jobs they can do with their human on weekends or after work. One of those jobs is "therapy dog."

CHAPTER 11

ANGEL
ON A LEASH

THE WESTMINSTER Kennel Club Dog Show holds a special place in the hearts of dog show exhibitors. People will tell you it is both the best and the worst dog show they attend each year. It's the best because so many beautiful dogs from all over the country are together in the same place; because it's the only time all year to catch up with friends from distant corners of the country; for networking with new acquaintances, as rounds of cocktail parties, banquets, charity balls, and art auctions, many with free drinks and meals, are paid for by Purina and Pedigree and Iams and other dog food companies. For social life, Westminster is the best.

It's the worst because as it is held in New York City in the second week of February when the weather is almost always terrible. A snowstorm may prevent you from arriving in Manhattan. Once you're at the show, a snowstorm may prevent you from leaving. Even if you go outside to brave the cold, wet, windy conditions, there's no place for your dog to pee. Taxis whiz by at 100 miles per hour and pedestrians practically knock you down on the street. Everyone is in a big hurry to get wherever it is they're going. Unless you're from New York City, it's jarring.

Westminster is also trying because every year a horrible, wheezing, hacking cough makes the rounds among the humans and a virus bug invades the intestines of the dogs. The dogs are stressed by long hours in their crates and the milling crowds who, although extremely friendly, stare unnervingly and try to pet them.

Nevertheless, it's America's most important dog show. The show has been held for 136 consecutive years, and is America's second-longest continuously staged sporting event. Like death and taxes, it is always there. Only the Kentucky Derby has been around longer.

Dogs who enter Westminster are at the top of their game. Sleek, fit, energetic, they are the best representatives of their breed and wonderful to behold. But sometimes the lights, cameras, and action of Westminster obscure part of the truth. Each one of these canines is not just a highly groomed and insanely coveted competitor. Each one is also *somebody's dog*.

Another great thing about Westminster. You get a chance to see breeds that may be extremely rare—for instance, the American Water Spaniel, a breed developed to hunt from land or dive out of boats in their native state of Wisconsin. The American Water Spaniel's marcel coat contains a natural oil that allows him easy passage through the water without getting bogged down. He is a powerful swimmer. And if you ran into dog owner Don Hancock at the bench of his American Water Spaniel, Rodney, you'd find that he is also a unique kind of therapy dog. His comforting 40 pounds were usually pressed right up against Don's leg.

Don had never thought about doing therapy dog work and had no plans to get Rodney involved in it. But one hot summer day, he and Rodney were visiting at a friend's swimming pool while an instructor was struggling to teach a class of young children to swim. It wasn't going well. The children were frightened, and they didn't want to go into the water. Once in, they didn't want to push off from the side.

Don was thinking how interesting it was that dogs are natural swimmers, but children are not. No one needs to teach a Water Spaniel how to push powerfully with his hind legs to keep himself afloat. And no one teaches him to use his front legs to paddle. The first time a Spaniel hits the water, he swims.

Don noticed that Rodney was watching the children intently. Maybe he was thinking the same thing. Of course, being human, he wasn't sure what Rodney thought of them.

On the other hand, it was clear what the kids thought of Rodney. They swarmed over him, petting and giggling, telling him he was a good dog. Most of them would rather stay on land and play with Rodney than try swimming.

Don urged Rodney to get into the pool. Rodney looked at him as though he'd lost his mind. Rodney was unafraid of deep water in fast-flowing channels. He was unflinching in carrying heavy game through a strong current back to shore. But this nice clean swimming pool with these screaming kids splashing around—he wanted no part of this.

But like all good dogs, Rodney was used to trusting his owner. So when Don insisted, Rodney got to his feet and with a worried look on his face, got in the pool. The frightened children were amazed. There was dark brown, 40-pound Rodney, close in size to one of them, swimming with ease from side to side. And no one had taught him how. He was just doing it. The swimming instructor saw the lesson to be learned here and urged the kids to follow Rodney. Rodney led the kids in short bursts down the side and back. He showed them how to cross the width of the pool while keeping their heads above the water. He demonstrated that water in the eyes and nose is not a big problem. Just give a good shake; problem solved. He insisted that despite what the children thought, swimming was good fun.

He took frequent breaks on the pool steps, but when called upon, valiantly demonstrated to every child what to do. He understood his role and buoyantly swam around as they doggy-paddled after him.

Rodney came to Westminster from Wisconsin with his uncle, Cowboy, and another relative. Cowboy was the eventual winner. Cowboy is an expert on hunting the most rare of grouse birds, the "ruffed grouse." He hails from Park Falls, Wisconsin, the self-proclaimed "Ruffed Grouse Capital of the World." Park Falls, according to the town's Web site, is the only township in Price County with two traffic lights. Coming to New York from Wisconsin's northern highlands, the two dogs probably felt they were coping with life on another, not particularly friendly, planet.

Then there was Champion Snowyridge Don't Fence Me In, a Norwich Terrier. If ever you are lost in the mountains of Santa Barbara, you'll want to have Dudley, as he's called, with you. Dudley knows how to warn about the approach of unfriendly wildlife. He took a rattlesnake avoidance class last spring in his hometown. One month after the class, he excitedly alerted his owner to a small chest in her bedroom. She thought he was fooling around and looking for a toy, but when she opened it, inside was a rattlesnake, whose poison would have been deadly if he had struck a member of the family. Dudley won Best of Breed at Westminster but was unimpressed with the medallion he took home. He was eager to get back on rattlesnake patrol.

Or consider the Australian Terrier, Champion Temora Bully for You. He won an Award of Merit at Westminster, but deserves a greater one for having taught himself to alert his owner, Julie

Seaton, when her diabetic son is about to have a hypoglycemic seizure. Even experts cannot train "alert dogs" because no one is sure what they are alerting to. Is it a change in smell caused by chemicals flooding the bloodstream? Or can they sense the approach of a seizure through the suddenly jumbled brainwaves in an epileptic human's aura?

Over at the Dachshund ring, another Award of Merit winner, Champion Brodny Schoolhouse Rocketman, was wagging his tail with eagerness to get out of the ring and into the arms of his owner, Josh Caporale. Lincoln is credited with providing the motivation for Josh to overcome some of the problems associated with autism. Lincoln's breeders, Fred and Carol Vogel, said they knew they were giving the boy a really fine show puppy, but they had promised him one. As the puppies grew, Link turned into a wonderful specimen of the breed. After handler Pam de Rosiers showed him to his championship, she asked Carol the question that haunts every show breeder at some point, "Why didn't you keep this one?"

The reputation of a dog breeder rises and falls on the quality of the stock that makes it into the show ring. Knowing that Link had the potential to be a big winner, the Vogels asked Josh if it would be okay to borrow Link back for a year, so he could go to shows. They invited Josh to come out from his Connecticut home any weekend to watch him.

Josh considered the matter carefully. He thought about the fact that he was entering high school and had been told he would be expected to work hard at his homework and activities. He decided that Lincoln's situation was similar; therefore Link should go out and work at getting good grades, or, in his case, ribbons, just as Josh was. He told his mother, "Link and I will both work hard this year doing our jobs."

At Westminster, his face was proud as Carol introduced him as Link's owner.

The Newfoundland who won Best in Show in 2004, Champion Darbydale's All Rise Pouch Cove, retired from the show ring that day and now visits nursing homes once a week with his owner, Dave Helming. Champion Felicity's Diamond Jim, the English Springer Spaniel who won Best in Show in 2007, loves his role as a therapy dog for Alzheimer's patients.

The stories of these dogs were uncovered by David Frei as he prepared the commentary for the television broadcast of the Westminster Dog Show. He said he's been heartened by the number of Westminster dog owners willing to give up time each week in order to do therapy work. He and his wife, Sherri, were early proponents of the therapy dog concept. He wrote an award-winning book titled *Angel by My Side*; gives talks to groups of dog lovers called "My Angel Has Four Legs"; and he's a hands-on person who, despite traveling in the higher echelons of the Manhattan business and social elite, makes time every Tuesday evening to take his Brittany Spaniels, Teigh and Belle, to Children's Hospital or Ronald McDonald House.

David Frei thought it would be a good idea to spread the therapy dog concept even farther. He came up with a plan. The prestigious Westminster Kennel Club should support therapy-dog work by starting its own charity. He had a name picked out: "Angel On A Leash."

Once the organization was up and running, he had Westminster honor one team each year by giving an award in front of the packed Madison Square Garden audience. In 2007, a tall woman named Gay Cropper was called to center stage, with a little one-eyed Brussels Griffon by her side. David read out the list of their accomplishments. This pair visited Children's Hospital every week for animal-assisted therapy. They worked with children who had cancer and heart failure and leukemia and broken bones. The little dog had a special knack for encouraging children who couldn't walk to stand up and give it a try. Even when the little dog lost an eye in an accident, he had missed only two weeks before getting back to work.

He had a long name for such a little dog, Mister Gruffyd Babayan.

⌒⌐

DURING THE YEARS that Gay Cropper was raising eight children on the Upper East Side of New York, she didn't pay a lot of attention to dogs. With two of her own kids and six step-children, her days were busy. The family had pet dogs, but Gay says she didn't understand people who said things like, "I can't come visit you because I don't want to put my dog in a kennel."

"I'd say, 'For heaven's sake, it's a *dog*. Just put it in the kennel and come visit me.'"

Gay had once entertained the idea of becoming a nurse. But now the thought makes her laugh. "I would have been terrible at it! I don't like blood. I wouldn't like cleaning up patients. It would not have been a good job for me."

Her husband, Harry, built a restaurant for her on 71st Street between York and First Avenues. The Harry & Me Café was popular with doctors and nurses from New York Hospital, just a block away. Gay remembers: "There was a bank president who came in several times a week. His wife told me, 'He refuses to go to any other restaurant. Just Harry & Me Café and Lutece. That's it.'"

As the hostess and the namesake of the restaurant, Gay had to be there all the time. But after four years, it had gotten to be too much. The eight kids at home had to come first.

Once the kids were grown and she and her husband were alone in the house, Gay acquired two dogs to keep her company—a Pit Bull/Lab/Boxer mix named Rudolph, and a Chihuahua. One day she stopped into the store Pets on Lex to buy dog food. She walked down the aisle, trying not to look at the puppies for sale, but looking anyway. "I just saw the ugliest dog I have ever seen in my life," she told two of her grandchildren when she got home. "He looked like a wizened old man, with very little hair and a funny, downturned face. He kept watching me wherever I went in the store."

When their parents came to pick them up, the children clamored, "Can we go to the store and see the ugly dog?"

"My son said, sure," Gay remembers. "That side of my family are dog lovers. He put us all in the car and we drove down."

Gay had been a lifelong advocate of getting dogs from the pound. But her daughter-in-law said: "That ugly dog keeps looking at you! He won't take his eyes off you!"

Her daughter-in-law told the clerk to let them hold the dog. When she handed him over to Gay, "He put his front legs around my neck and wouldn't let go. It was embarrassing. I tried to leave. I couldn't get the dog off me. They told me how much he was and I said, 'That's ridiculous.' I said, 'I don't have money with me anyway. Let's go.' My son said, 'Mom, I have a charge card.' That's how I ended up with him."

The ugly dog was a Brussels Griffon, and the name that was soon attached to him was Mr. Gruffyd Babayan. Now Gay had three dogs to walk in the park, where she'd meet up with other dog owners. One young woman told her excitedly that she'd signed up her Lab for therapy dog work. She wanted Gay to get Mr. Gruffyd Babayan involved. "She said, 'He'd be great with kids. Just looking at him makes people smile.' I laughed. I told her, 'He would never be able to do that. He won't do anything I say. He's the least obedient dog in the world.'"

But her friend had put Gay's name on the list to attend a lecture, so she went along to the ASPCA that weekend. Trainers from the Delta Society talked about the training and commitment that would be required from a therapy dog team. An elegant, stylishly dressed woman named Greer Griffith told them about Angel On A Leash, her chapter of the Delta Society, sponsored by David Frei and the Westminster Kennel Club. Gay didn't know it then, but the Delta Society is a pioneer dog-therapy field. The organization's training and requirements are the most rigorous in the nation. David Frei, who now works as a Delta Society spokesman, describes them as "the Cadillac of the therapy dog industry."

At the end of the talk, trainers were administering tests to dogs who had taken the course, so they could become certified. One person had canceled, so the trainers were left with one open spot. Gay asked hesitantly: "Could I take the test with my dog? I'll flunk, but then I will know whether or not we could do this. I don't think my dog would be any good at it."

Mr. Gruffyd Babayan passed perfectly.

With no training, Gay's new dog did everything a potential therapy canine was supposed to do. Everything. Perfectly. He stayed at the end of the leash while Gay walked away. He sat on command, ignored food put down to tempt him, and ignored the intrusion of other dogs. When put on the laps of three different people in wheelchairs, he sat quietly while they petted him or were rough with him. He responded to all the basic commands. He qualified.

Gay was floored. At home, she asked him to repeat those behaviors; sit, stay, and ignore food. "He looked at me like, 'Are you crazy?' He would never dream of doing that."

But the conclusion was obvious. Mr. Gruffyd Babayan was meant to be a therapy dog. At least, he seemed to think so.

Gay signed up for the training because the Delta Society is very strict about requirements. You must take a course, complete a home study, and the dog needs a complete physical. He must pass a temperament test, a Pet Partners Aptitude Test, and a Pet Partners Skills Test.

That done, Gay and her dog were qualified to do what Gay

calls "the meet-and-greet." They went with two other teams to the pediatric floor of Morgan Stanley Children's Hospital Presbyterian/New York. The head nurse handed each of them a list of names and rooms of children who could be visited. Doctor's permission is required, because they don't visit any child who may have a weak immune system or contagious infection.

When Gay looked at her list, the first name was a child she knew—her best friend's four-year-old grandson. He was scheduled for a heart operation. It seemed significant that her first visit would be to help a child she knew.

The little boy was delighted to receive a visit from Mr. Gruffyd Babayan. The whole family was there; parents, siblings, grandparents, aunts, cousins. The hospital was generous with visiting arrangements, Gay discovered—she visited one room containing fifteen relatives and friends. Everywhere she went, everyone smiled at the sight of the ugly canine ambassador.

That first night, she boosted Mr. Gruffyd Babayan onto the bed of a boy who was eating a hamburger. Later, when a Delta trainer heard about that, she scolded Gay. Don't put him in a situation where he would be so tempted to misbehave, she said. It's very hard for a dog to ignore a hamburger. But Mr. G.B. had no problem with it. Gay says: "When he's working, he just knows he is meant to be very quiet and calm. He always does the right thing. Nobody has to tell him."

Delta Society requires that teams spend only about an hour at the hospital, because they don't want the dogs to become stressed and overtired. So Gay and Mr. G.B. spent about ten minutes with each child. As she was preparing to leave, a father came into the hallway to speak with her.

"You people are saints," he said. His child had been at the hospital for a year. The therapy dog visits were one of the highlights of his son's week.

Gay thought, He's going a little overboard. We're not that wonderful. It's nice, but I don't know that it makes a huge difference. It's fun for the kids. That's all.

Gay and Mr. G.B. started a regular weekly schedule: Morgan Stanley Children's Hospital on Tuesday nights and Ronald Mc-Donald House on Fridays. Mr. G.B. couldn't read a calendar, but he quickly learned to tell what day it was. When his tall, elegant mistress laid out a nice outfit for herself on the bed and pulled his green Delta Society scarf from a drawer, he would start barking madly and race through the house. Gay thought, No one would believe this dervish of a dog was the careful, obedient animal who positioned himself so gently next to sick children.

In fact, she says, when she gets out a nice outfit for another reason, maybe to meet a friend for lunch, Mr. G.B. is annoyed. He can't see the point of Gay dressing up if the two of them are not heading to the hospital. The Delta Society requires dogs have a bath before every visit. Mr. G.B. is personally opposed to that regulation, but he knows that when he takes a bath, he's going to work. So he puts up with it.

He gets sad if he doesn't see the kids for more than four days in a row. He looks at Gay in despair. Why aren't we going? Did you forget?

The Delta Pet Partners are not allowed to ask what's wrong with any of the children. So unless the child or parent wants to talk about it, Gay doesn't know. She finds lots of things to talk to the kids about that don't involve illness. Did you ever have a dog? If you could have a dog, what kind would you have? Mr. Gruffyd Babayan's name alone is always a source of conversation. It's a long name, Gay likes to say, but Mr. G.B. likes it that way. If you don't use the whole name, he just looks at you and waits until you say it. Can you say it?

The kids can say it right after one or two tries, but often the parents can't. The kids love that.

Sometimes Gay tells them how she came to get Mr. G. B., or

how they got started in therapy work. Mr. G.B. has his own business card, which tells his name, age, breed, and describes his favorite game as "Catch Me if You Can." In fact, Greer makes up business cards for each of the Angel On A Leash dogs, and kids collect them as if they were Pokémon or baseball cards.

After more coursework and testing, Gay and Mr. G.B. graduated to "Animal-Assisted Therapy Dog." Now, instead of "meet-and-greet," Gay and her Griff were scheduled to go to the physical therapy department and get a specific assignment.

Gay wasn't sure how Mr. Gruffyd Babayan would handle this. It was one thing to sit in laps and tend to bedridden children. This new assignment would require that he follow commands: walk, stay, lie down, and things like that. He had a policy of not following commands. So on their first day, Gay was full of trepidation.

The therapist explained that they needed to get an eight-year-old girl up on her feet. She refused to use the bars to hold herself up and walk because she was in pain. The girl wanted to be left alone. The therapist pointed to the bars and said, "Can you make him back up along here, and I'll get her to follow?"

Gay looked dubiously at her Brussels Griffon. "I don't think so," she said. "He's never done anything like that. I don't think he can walk backward."

The therapist was disappointed. She'd seen other dogs do the maneuver. "Okay, then, just get him to walk there, any way you can. Maybe she'll follow."

The little girl with long brown hair wore a blue hospital gown, but Gay could see that both legs were bandaged. The girl's eyes sparkled when she saw Mr. Gruffyd Babayan, but she winced when she tried to stand. She was enchanted by Mr. G.B. and reached out toward him, and the therapist directed her arms onto the bars. As Gay wondered how to direct Mr. Gruffyd Babayan, he moved past her and stood directly in front of the girl. Their eyes locked. Then Mr. Gruffyd Babayan backed up.

Gay tried to pretend she wasn't shocked. He'd never backed up in his life, as far as she knew. Backing up is not a natural movement for a dog, who has four legs to coordinate.

The little girl took a step forward; Mr. G.B. took a step back. Then they repeated the maneuver. They moved all the way down the bars that way. At the end, the little girl was allowed to sit and clasp Mr. G.B. to her chest.

On another visit, the therapist asked Gay if she could get Mr. Gruffyd Babayan to stand and sit, in order to encourage a little girl to do it. Gay shook her head sadly. "He doesn't know the command to stand," she said. "He's never done anything like that."

The therapist asked the little girl to sit and stand fifteen times, but she didn't even want to do it once. Mr. G.B. was on the platform next to her, and she was promised she could play with him after her therapy. The therapist asked her gently, "Okay, now, stand up."

To the surprise of both Gay and the therapist, when Mr. Gruffyd Babayan heard the words "Stand up," he did. So did the little girl. "Sit" he knew. They both sat. Then they began to stand up and sit down with each command—fifteen times, in unison. The therapist gave Gay a quizzical look. She shrugged her shoulders. Mr. Gruffyd Babayan was making a liar out of her. "I've tried to ask him to 'stand' many times," Gay insists. "He looks at me like, 'Are you crazy?'"

Two years into their work, Mr. Gruffyd Babayan had an accident that could have meant an end to his volunteer sessions. He was home, running through the house, when he crashed into a flight of steps and damaged his eye. Gay rushed him to the vet, where the veterinarian told her he would have to go into surgery immediately. He would lose the eye.

It was an incident that might have crushed a lesser team. But two weeks after his surgery, Mr. G.B. was back, the skin stitched closed over his empty eye socket. Gay refused to let anyone feel sorry for him. She used his accident as a story to share with the kids, telling them that Mr. G.B. had been in the hospital with an IV-drip in his leg and not even his mommy and daddy could visit him. Then she'd show the place on his front leg where the doctors had shaved away the hair to put the IV in.

She'd tell them he had been scared, but he was a brave patient while he was in the hospital. Just like you.

One night, their visiting list included a seven-year-old boy who had accidentally fallen out of a fifth-floor window. Only movement would loosen up the injured boy's muscles, but he resisted because every movement hurt. They asked Gay to try to get the boy to brush Mr. G.B.'s red hair.

When they walked into the room, the little boy's jaw dropped. He kept staring at Mr. Gruffyd Babayan. Finally he asked the dog, "What floor did you fall out of?"

Gay said Mr. G.B. had hurt himself racing around at home. The boy said, "I fell out the fifth floor." It was the first time the boy had willingly spoken about the accident, even with his family. The doctors wanted him to talk because he had been retreating into depressed silence.

Gay and Mr. G.B. have visited hundreds, eventually thousands of children with heart transplants, liver transplants, bone marrow transplants, cancer, leukemia, diabetes, and brain tumors. They've seen children with abdominal pain, bladder infections, scratched eyes, and crushed hands. One little girl had a rare condition in which her organs were too big for her body—they were growing too fast and causing terrible pain.

Another time, a therapist asked Gay to help with a fourteen-year-old boy who was waiting for a heart to become available for transplant. The doctors needed him to move, but working with him would be very delicate. His blood was being pumped through a box, which a specialist had to monitor constantly. Because of his condition it was necessary to keep his blood pressure stable, but moving always made a person's pressure rise. And, to make things more difficult, the boy had only one leg. But keeping him moving and active would increase the chance of success for his operation. It was a dilemma.

Gay brought Mr. G.B. in, but it seemed to her the boy was not very interested. The therapist asked him to pet Mr. G.B., and he did, but seemed disaffected. Then she asked him to get up and use the walker. Gay noticed how all the medical people in the room seemed to stiffen with dread. It made her think they must have tried this before, without success.

It required four medical people plus Gay and Mr. Gruffyd Babayan to move with the boy. Mr. G.B. was patient, moving a step and letting the boy catch up, then moving again. After they'd gone down the corridor, the nurse with the blood pressure monitor cried out, "Hey! What's going on?" and everyone jolted to a halt.

The therapist asked anxiously, "What's happening?"

The nurse was flustered. "His blood pressure is not going up," she said. "I'm waiting for it to go up, but it hasn't changed. I'm wondering if the blood pressure cuff is broken."

The therapist smiled, relieved. "It's not broken," she said. "That's the dog. It's the effect of the dog."

There were several converts that day to the advantages of Animal-Assisted Therapy. One of them was Gay. She said, "Sometimes you know the dog is making a difference. This time, until the nurse spoke, I didn't think it was."

She says she sometimes asks herself, "'Why do you do this?' It's pretty painful. And I realize this work is so fulfilling because I'm not asked to fix anything. I'm not asked to make anything better. I'm just asked to make them smile or move a little bit. It's not that much to do. But it makes so much difference."

Gay says, "I never wanted to volunteer anywhere because I felt too self-conscious. I didn't think I could be the person who said, 'I can offer you something.' But when it's the dog, it's not focused on me. I'm just the chauffeur. So I'm able to be bold.

"I was never able to do interviews or be on TV," Gay continues. "If you were giving me an award for being the best woman in the world, I probably would say, 'I don't want it because I don't want to be interviewed.' The first time they asked me if I would do an interview about Angel On A Leash for a magazine article, I said, 'Oh no, I can't.' Then I thought, 'It's not me they're interested in—they're interested in the dog.' So the next time they asked I said, 'Okay.' I can be brave because it's for the dog. It's not me."

If it sounds like this has been a positive experience for Gay Cropper, she would agree.

"It's the most transforming thing that ever happened to me. It makes me feel worthwhile in a way that is so ridiculously simple. It made me realize that the reason I wanted to be a nurse was because you can make a big difference in someone's life."

Gay checks the time and rises to her feet. "My dog is working tonight, so I'm not free to sit down and have a long conversation. I have to bathe him and get him ready."

Sometimes she thinks about that father who spoke to her on their first visit, saying, "You people are saints." She still doesn't think they're saints. "It's not a huge burden. It doesn't kill us to do it. We have a nice time working together. And I don't have to take the credit. It's the dog."

⌒

MY TRANSLATOR, ELADIA, leads me from the IRT subway stop up Lexington Avenue to 111th Street in New York City. This neighborhood of Manhattan is El Barrio, or Spanish Harlem, and I'm apprehensive because I've never been here before. It's mid-afternoon. As we walk down the warm street at mid-day, the brownstones on either side of us have a dusty, weathered look, their blinds closed against the day as if they've seen too much. We pass one of the depressingly few trees, its trunk cut with hearts and initials and vows of undying love. A group of screaming ten-year-old girls runs by us, their rucksacks bouncing against their shoulders, their dark hair streaming in the breeze.

In this section of New York, produce bins are overflowing with plantains, calabasa melons, and chayote squash. Fast-food centers display tamales and burritos. Proportionally there are far more beauty salons per block than in any other part of Manhattan. Bodegas on every corner are plastered with ads for Corona *cerveza* and Kool.

Rounding a corner, Eladia points out a four-story building up ahead. The woman I wish to meet lives in apartment 4A; I pray there will be an elevator. There is not. Eladia, dainty and twenty-six, skips lightly up the steps. I trudge behind her. We reach the door of 4A and she smiles at me as she knocks. The door is drawn open by a thin, small, olive-skinned woman, who must be Carmelita Rodríguez Oron.

Eladia breaks into an explanation in lilting Spanish in which I recognize only the words for "hospital," "doctors," therapy," "daughter," "writer," and "dog." Carmelita tucks a few strands of hair under a blue paisley kerchief as she listens. Her dark eyes, when she glances up at me, look soft and confused. Through a quick conversation with Eladia, I ask if we could perhaps hear about her child's experience in the hospital.

She asks if the hospital sent me. I try to get Eladia to explain carefully that they did not. Under the rules of privacy, the hospital may not tell me anything about any of the patients. Through a tangled route, I found a charitable organization and a woman, Anna, who is Carmelita's friend. If Carmelita doesn't want to talk to me, we'll go away.

At last she opens the door fully and beckons us inside. The apartment is small and holds a mixture of worn-out furniture and colorful new toys. We must be quiet because Carmelita's *nieta*, her granddaughter, is sleeping.

With a deep sigh, Carmelita begins the story. Her granddaughter, Antonia, is five years old. Her birthday, May 15, is soon approaching. When she was born, her mother, Juana, Carmelita's daughter, was a heroin addict. At first, Antonia was a beautiful child, and completely normal in every way. She smiles at the memory.

But when she was four, Tonia fell down. She said that her back hurt. It started to hurt all the time. Then she couldn't walk. Juana took her to the emergency room twice and the doctors did nothing. The third time, a smart doctor realized there *was* something wrong with the girl and sent her to a specialist at Children's Hospital of New York. X-rays, an MRI, and other tests were taken. They injected dye in her spine and took pictures. They wanted to take Juana's blood for tests but Juana got scared and left for Puerto Rico. She is staying in San Juan with her aunt and uncle and working as a maid at a resort hotel.

The story about Juana becomes clear to us only later, after we dissect Carmelita's story. We think she was telling us that Juana is afraid that her drug use caused her daughter's problems.

"It was a tumor," Carmelita says gravely. She makes a circle with her index finger that looks rather small. But a tumor this size is a terrible thing in a little girl's spine. The doctors explained the problem in solemn tones. They wanted to operate and remove the tumor. But no one could promise that Tonia would walk. The operation's success rate was about fifty-fifty.

The operation took more than six hours. It was an extremely delicate one because one tiny slip of the scalpel could have severed the nerves in the spinal column, which would have caused permanent paralysis to the legs. Tonia had to stay in the hospital for many days.

Carmelita visited her every day, before and after her shift as a shirt presser at the Mr. Clean dry cleaner. At Our Lady Queen of Angels Church, Father Peron took up a collection to help her pay

Tonia's bills. Carmelita prayed to St. Jude and also to St. Rose of Lima for a miracle. She smiles as she tells me this, blesses herself, and pulls a silver cross around her neck up to her lips to kiss it.

The surgeons said the operation was a success. They wanted Tonia to begin physical therapy, but she didn't want to. She was unhappy. She had a lot of pain-killing drugs in her system. She wanted her mother.

The physical therapists tried to get Tonia to move her legs, but she wouldn't. She said she couldn't, but the doctors thought her legs were okay. She had feeling, so the nerves had not been cut. But day after day, Tonia did not stand. They had crutches for her, but she would only ride in the wheelchair. Carmelita begged her to try to stand but she wouldn't do it.

One day, the physical therapist came to the room and said she had a surprise. A special person would visit Tonia in the therapy center. Her grandmother tried to interest her but Tonia said she didn't care, not unless it was her mother.

When they got to therapy, the physical therapist introduced them to a nice woman with a big yellow dog. Carmelita didn't remember the dog's name or what breed it was. Tonia could only remember that he was a bouncy dog and she was frightened of him. The therapist urged her to stroke him and touch his ears, but Tonia didn't want to. Around Tonia's home neighborhood, she knew mostly Pit Bulls. This was not a Pit Bull, but she still was apprehensive. She had been instructed to keep her distance from big dogs. She really didn't want to go near this one.

❧

THE NEXT TIME, Tonia went down to the therapy floor with another little girl, Mary. There was a very small reddish-brown dog there. He worked with Mary. Tonia was fascinated. Like Tonia, Mary had to relearn how to walk. She got up on the walking bars. The little dog was in front of her, and he backed up, then Mary took a step. Then he backed up again, and she took another step. Tonia and her *abuelita* just watched. Nobody made Tonia try. But then the woman with the dog came over and sat with Tonia. The little dog got up next to her and put his head on her lap. She stroked his brown hair and tickled his silly little ears. She told him he looked like a silly spider. After awhile, the "spider's" owner asked if she wanted to try the walking bars with the "spider" helping her and Tonia said okay. She copied Mary. The little dog went in front, backed up one step, and sat down. Then Tonia took one step. The dog backed another step, Tonia did another one. Tonia and the dog together covered the entire ramp in this fashion.

Then, whenever Tonia went to physical therapy, this little dog was there, too. And it worked, because Tonia started walking right from that day. She stopped being so depressed. She was still a little depressed, but she didn't mind doing therapy.

To me, it seems simply amazing that a little dog succeeded in a situation where a therapist could not to motivate a five-year-old to walk. Carmelita does not share my wonder. To her it is all one: the amazing doctors, the operation that could have failed, the machine that tracks dye in her granddaughter's spine, the collection from Our Lady Queen of Angels, the social worker who got the state to pay for the operation. All of it has overwhelmed her. The technical advances and the dog's job as therapist are part of the same unknowable universe and do not inspire awe in her the way they do me. She has run out of a lifetime supply of awe. She feels that if I want to parse out the animal's role and reflect on it, that's my business. She will get on with her job at the dry cleaner. She will take Tonia to kindergarten. She will contemplate how to persuade her daughter to be a mother to Tonia again. She has a lot on her mind.

I ask if I may meet Tonia? Carmelita motions me to follow her to a closed door. Behind the door, in bed with fluffy white pillows and a pink quilt, a little angel is playing with a doll. Her hair is rumpled. She has just woken up. But she is as beautiful a being as has ever walked the earth. She has perfect little fingers and toes and a radiant smile. She asks to get up, and her grandmother gets out a pink T-shirt and white skirt.

Tonia answers my questions in English. Does she remember the little dog? Of course! The little devil dog! He likes tuna fish. She giggles when she remembers him. He was a very funny-looking dog.

Eladia asks the grandmother if she remembers the dog's name. She rolls her eyes. It was a long, highly strange European-sounding name. The grandmother doesn't remember it because she could never pronounce it, not even when they told her what it was. So they just called him "the devil dog."

My translator, Eladia, is concerned for me. How can I write my story if no one remembers the dog's name? I tell her not to worry. I know the name. I met the devil dog at an elegant cocktail party in a new designer hotel on the Upper East Side of Manhattan, where he was being honored for his work with children like Tonia.

"Was the dog's name 'Mr. Gruffyd Babayan'?" I ask.

Her eyes light up and she claps her hands. "Mr. Gruffyd Babayan!" she cries, and does a little spinning dance around the floor.

Even though she couldn't remember his name, Antonia Diaz is one of Mr. Gruffyd Babayan's success stories. He won't be resting on his laurels, however. He'll be back in the hospital next week, to see if there is another little girl in need of his special brand of encouragement.

Mr. Gruffyd Babayan is so earnest and hardworking, he gives the impression he'd do anything to help his sick little friends. At the same time that Mr. Gruffyd Babayan was urging his injured charges to walk, other dogs working with other humans in other parts of the country had figured out a highly canine way to come up with a diagnosis for a terrible human illness.

CHAPTER 12

THE WOMAN WIIO SMELLED LIKE CANCER

IN 1989 A LETTER to the editor appeared in *The Lancet*, the highly respected British medical journal. The headline read: "Sniffer Dogs in the Melanoma Clinic?"

Two London dermatologists wrote about a case in which a patient had been sent to them by her dog. According to the letter, the woman had a dark spot on her upper leg that her doctor said was a mole, a small, slightly raised blemish on the skin, made dark by a high concentration of melanin. Purely a cosmetic matter, not worth removing.

The woman was content with that diagnosis. But her dog was not. Her dog, a half–Border Collie, half–Doberman Pinscher, would not stop sniffing the mole on her leg. She would push her nose into her skirt or pants, and sniff heavily at the spot, always interrupting and bothering her. No matter how many times she ordered her dog to stop, the canine kept coming back. At first, she laid the whole thing off to an obnoxious dog and her own bad dog training.

Then came the startling moment one summer day when she decided to work in her garden in shorts. This meant the mole was exposed. Her dog pounced on her and nipped at the mole, trying to bite it off. She had to push her strongly to get her away. That shocked her. Her dog had never attacked or bitten her before. In reconsidering the incident, the woman realized that she had other moles on her body, but the dog completely ignored these. Why did her dog show such fervent interest in only this mole? Why would she act so strangely?

Maybe something else was wrong. She insisted on being referred to a dermatological specialist. During her examination, the doctors excised the mole and sent it to the lab for biopsy. The results came back, "Positive." The mole was cancerous. It was a malignant melanoma, measuring 1.86 in thickness, a deadly form of skin cancer, which could have spread rapidly and killed her if she had not taken action to stop it.

"This dog may have saved her owner's life by prompting her to seek treatment when the lesion was still at a thin and curable stage," wrote the researchers, Drs. H. Williams and A. Pembroke. Their conclusion was that her cancer must have had a scent that her dog identified as harmful to its own. The doctors thought that studies should be done to confirm this.

Florida. Four years later. A Tallahassee dermatologist, Dr. Armand Cognetta, was driving home from a long day at work, thinking about a patient. Dr. Cognetta specializes in skin cancer, working eleven-hour days, seeing more than 100 patients a week. It's hard work because the primary tool a doctor uses to diagnose skin cancer is the human eye. And the visual difference between a cancerous and a noncancerous mole is—well, sometimes there's no difference at all. Subtle changes in color or shape can indicate the presence of a melanoma, but sometimes such changes in moles turn out to be nonmelanoma. Additionally, there are many different kinds of skin cancer; each is manifested differently depending upon the afflicted individual. Even today, it's estimated that physicians may miss 30 percent of malignant melanomas.

That afternoon, Dr. Cognetta had done a biopsy of a very tiny mole he'd found on one of his patients. It was neither dark, strangely colored, nor oddly shaped. It didn't have any of the definitive signs of cancer, yet under the microscope, he saw that it was. The thought that he could have missed such a small cancer put him on edge. He kept thinking, "What's a better way?"

While he drove, he listened to a news story about how police had recovered the body of a missing swimmer from a lake. They had not used poles or scuba gear; instead, they had a cadaver dog sit in the bow of the boat, using his powerful sense of smell to sniff the air. The dog led them to the body.

The thought hit him; if a dog could find a body under several feet of water, could a dog find cancer? What did cancer smell like? Could a dog distinguish between a normal mole and a cancerous one?

When he searched medical literature for any mention of melanoma and scent, all he could find was the five-paragraph letter to the editor in The Lancet. That was it. There was no sign that anyone had followed up on the doctors' story.

Dr. Cognetta decided to try. He contacted Duane Pickel, an expert dog trainer and former head of the Tallahassee Police K-9 Department, whom he knew because Pickel had trained the dogs of several of his friends. Pickel volunteered to train his own dog, George, a Standard Schnauzer, who was already highly successful in detecting bombs and explosive devices.

Pickel had George retrieve PVC (polyvinyl chloride) tubes that contained samples of melanoma. For a pro like George that command was no problem. Then, Pickel started hiding the tubes before sending George to retrieve them. George had to search the room, looking under the desk, behind the sofa, on a bookshelf, to find the tube. When he brought it to Pickel, he got a reward. Then, he asked George to pick out which one of ten identical tubes contained the melanoma sample.

George could do it every time.

Next, they recruited Kim Edwards, RN, head nurse of the out-patient surgical unit at Tallahassee Memorial Regional Medical Center. With a family history of skin cancer, she found the idea of early detection of the disease to be highly appealing.

Pickel designed a special low table, just at George's sniffing height, for Kim to lie on. A number of bandages were taped to her body; only one bandage contained a sample of melanoma. This test was important because it would show George's ability to tell the difference between healthy human skin and diseased skin.

In preparation, Kim had washed in Ivory soap and tried not to wear any kind of scent. But even so, there would be many more odors on a human body than George had encountered in the tubes.

The melanoma was under the bandage on Kim's right shoulder. Pickel gave George the command to find the cancer. George walked around Kim's body, sniffing carefully; there were bandages on her feet, her knees, and her stomach. George ignored all of them, until he reached her right shoulder. He sniffed at it, and then he sat and looked at Pickel.

Pickel said, "Show me," and George then lifted his paw and touched the bandage. The team was elated—it was the break-through they had hoped for. Pickel had been confident in George's abilities from the start. But for the others, George's success proved without question that it was possible that a dog could detect cancer.

Kim was tested for several more weeks. In some of the tests

there were no traces of melanoma on Kim at all; this was done in order to see if there was any possibility George was guessing. But on those tests, he simply returned to Pickel. He never gave a false positive. When George's success rate again approached 100 percent, it was time for the next step.

Dr. Cognetta recruited patients who had been examined, but whose diagnoses had not yet been determined concerning cancer. Dr. Cognetta managed to find seven people who agreed to be sniffed by George. On five of the patients, George indicated the presence of melanoma. On a sixth patient, George indicated melanoma on a patient in a location where the subsequent lab test did not find evidence of cancer. Before marking this result as a "false positive," the doctors decided to retest the patient. The second test found melanoma in just a fraction of the cells. The first test had missed it because the cancerous area was so tiny. But George had not missed it. George had been right all along.

On a seventh patient, there was no definitive finding of cancer—from the doctors, from the lab, and from George. But later re-examination of that patient found a melanoma.

At this point, Pickel had trained a second dog, a Golden Retriever named Breeze, to do the same work. When she sniffed patients, she gave the exact same answers that George had.

The dogs had a higher success rate than doctors and a higher success rate than laboratory tests.

Dr. Cognetta hoped a research institution might pursue the matter, but no one came forward. In fact, when his results became known, he found himself the center of many unkind jokes and sneers. Newspaper headlines didn't help, with banners like, "Dr. Dog," "The Dog Will See You Now," "Dog Replaces Doctor," and "Diagnosis? Ask the Dog." His colleagues didn't take the study's results seriously. Mainstream science wasn't interested. The entire project seemingly faded away.

That was until 2002, when Dr. Jim Walker, head of the Sensory Research Institute at Florida State University, was fascinated to discover that this important research had been accomplished right in his own hometown, Tallahassee. Dr. Walker is an expert on the subject of dogs and smells. Having spent his entire career studying the relationship between the two, Dr. Walker designed and ran a study to find out just how good a dog's sense of smell truly is. He also was tired of hearing offhand remarks that dogs could smell ten times better than humans, or fifty times, or a hundred. No one really knew because no one had gone through the methodology to find out.

So Dr. Walker set out to do just that. First, he found the threshold at which a human could smell a scent. Then he set about finding the threshold to a dog's abilities. He was using n-amyl acetate (nAA), a chemical that he diluted one part to ten, then one to one hundred, then one to one thousand, and so on. Dr. Walker documented the fact that a dog can detect chemicals at one ten-thousandth to one one-hundred-thousandth the concentrations that humans can. In other words, at a minimum, dogs can smell 10,000 times better than a human. This research was published in *Applied Animal Behavior Science* as an article, "Naturalistic Quantification of Canine Olfactory Sensitivity."

When Dr. Walker discovered the work of Dr. Cognetta and Duane Pickel, he was stunned. "It takes a lot of courage to initiate a study outside the realm of what everybody thinks is 'normal' science," he said. "There were tremendous pressures on them not to do this. In my opinion, these people are heroes. They showed us what could be done."

The first team had only been guessing that cancer had a particular smell, which dogs could detect. But Dr. Walker knew from his work that it did. As cancer cells break down healthy cells, gas chromatography had shown that traces of saturated hydrocarbons such as alkanes and benzene derivatives and minute amounts of formaldehyde are released. Since dogs can detect chemicals in concentrations as small as a few parts per trillion, Dr. Walker thought dogs would most likely be able to detect these substances.

〜

DR. WALKER REALIZED that what had been missing from the 1994 study team was a scientist, such as himself, who could put the research into the format accepted by professional journals. Dr. Walker and his wife, Diane, also a "scent scientist," turned the first team's findings into a solid scientific article that was published in *Applied Animal Behavior Science* titled "Evidence of Canine Olfactory Detection of Melanoma." Both the press and the public loved the idea that dogs could detect cancer. Once again, the study made headlines around the world.

But once again, scientists and doctors scoffed at the idea. They couldn't see the point of research that involved a dog. Frustrated, Dr. Walker said to one of his doubting colleagues, who was about to fly to the Cayman Islands for a vacation, "When you get on that plane, do you want to know that bomb-detecting dogs went through the luggage?" The colleague immediately said, "Yes." But that still didn't convince him that dogs in a medical setting were worthwhile. Dr. Walker found that many scientists continued to doubt that dogs had the ability to pick up the scent of cancer.

However, 4,000 miles away, in Cambridge, England, a retired orthopedic surgeon named Dr. John Church was intrigued with Dr. Walker's findings. "I heard a report about this American fellow who trained his Schnauzer to pick out malignant skin lesions," he said. "I thought that was quite creative." Dr. Church was not afraid to fly in the face of medical convention to research something out of the ordinary. (He had been involved in a study that used maggots to clean infected wounds on human skin.)

He had also seen the letter to the editor in *The Lancet*. And he'd been collecting anecdotal stories about dogs who could detect cancer.

* A forty-four-year-old woman went to the doctor when her pet Dachshund wouldn't stop nudging one spot on her breast. The doctors discovered a cancerous tumor.

* A Dalmatian named Trudii owned by Gillian Lacey kept bothering a mole on her young owner's leg, even trying to nip it off. Medical examination revealed melanoma that required extensive surgery.

* Mike Holman from Reading, in Berkshire, complained to doctors that his Labrador Retriever, Parker, was showing inordinate interest in a patch of what he thought was eczema on his leg. "He was concentrating really hard and his tail would stop wagging," he said. This "eczema" turned out to be basal cell carcinoma. The dog had discovered it weeks or months or even years before it had become enough of a problem to cause concern. The dog's insistence on paying attention to that spot meant that Mike Holman did not lose his life to cancer that year.

Dr. Church and his team designed tests in which dogs were used to identify which urine samples came from patients who had cancer; six of the dogs in the tests were pets of team members: three Cocker Spaniels, a Labrador Retriever, a Papillon, and a mixed breed. The dog trainers came from a charity that trained dogs to work with people with hearing disabilities. The dogs were given seven months of training and then asked to pick out which of the urine samples contained cancer cells.

The results of Dr. Church's study were published in the *British Medical Journal* on September 28, 2004, which the doctors called "the first-ever meticulously controlled, double blind, peer-reviewed study on the subject."

Dr. Church wrote that the study was conclusive. Dogs could be trained to detect bladder cancer on the basis of urine odor alone. As a group, his dogs had correctly selected the right urine on twenty-two out of fifty four occasions, giving an average success rate of 41 percent. By chance alone, they'd be accurate one-seventh, or 14 percent, of the time.

The two best dogs, Tangle and Biddy, both Cocker Spaniels, were right 56 percent of the time, according to their trainer, Andrew Cook. The Papillon, Eliza, tied with Bea, the third Cocker Spaniel, followed by the Labrador, Jade. Bringing up the rear was Toddy, the mixed breed. "Bless him, he was working at a rate no better than chance, really, but we still love him," Cook said.

One of the cancer patients was identified correctly by all six dogs, whereas two other cancer patients were consistently missed, indicating that perhaps the strength of the urine signal varies from person to person.

Back at FSU, Dr. Walker thought the results were rather disappointing. "I hypothesize that dogs are phenomenally better than that," he said. He noted some of the variables in the British study, for instance, the dogs had no previous experience. They were not trained bomb detectors, accustomed to working with their noses, as George had been. And they had been given very little training.

But there was one thing that had happened during the training phase of the study that stunned everyone. The dogs were sniffing samples that the doctors knew came from people who had bladder cancer. The control samples came from people who did not. But one day, all the dogs alerted to one of the "clean" samples.

The trainers tried to train the dogs past that sample, telling the dogs they were wrong and urging them to look for the cancerous one. Yet time and again, the dogs disobeyed and alerted to the clean sample.

One of the doctors looked up the donor and asked him to come in for further testing, which showed, sure enough, that the man had a life-threatening tumor in his right kidney. Neither his doctor nor the laboratory test had picked up on it. But the dogs had. The dogs had been right. The patient was able to get treatment at an early stage so that the prognosis was good.

"As you can guess, we were cock-a-hoop about that," Dr. Church told a newspaper reporter from the British daily The Guardian.

Dr. Church said of his study: "This is a first step in the right direction. We regard this as a great breakthrough. I personally see a day when you could use dogs to detect disease. You've got a marvelous asset. You've got a wonderful tool."

He pointed out that prostate cancer kills 10,000 British men every year, and there is no easy way to detect it. The current test, the prostate specific antigen, is notoriously inaccurate, meaning it often says a man doesn't have cancer when in fact he does. A better test for this disease would save thousands of lives.

In 2000, another branch of the experimental tree sprung up in San Anselmo, California. The co-founders of the Pine Street Clinic, Dr. Michael McCulloch and Dr. Nicolas Broffman, had heard about the results of tests involving George the Schnauzer, and they'd met Dr. Walker at a conference on scent at the Florida Sensory Research Institute. The Pine Street Clinic is an institution committed to investigating any alternative or experimental therapy to help patients beat cancer. They believed that minute scents of lung cancer and breast cancer must be carried on a person's breath, but as yet this was unproven because there was no way at the time to measure and determine scientifically.

McCulloch and Broffman consulted with Dr. Walker, and set about proving it. The doctors obtained an apricot Standard Poodle from Canada, named Shing Ling, and started her with a dog trainer, Kirk Turner, when she was only nine weeks old.

They had their patients breathe deeply and exhale into tubes filled with polypropylene wool. Then the tubes were sealed. Kirk Turner taught Shing Ling to sniff the tubes. When she reached a tube known to contain the breath of a cancer patient, he clicked and gave her a treat. It's a positive training method that most dogs find a lot of fun. After many repetitions, Shing Ling became an outstanding detector of cancer.

She was right 99 percent of the time, a percentage believed by dog trainers and K-9 handlers the world over, but scoffed at by people in the medical and scientific communities.

"Their figures are simply too good to be true," one doctor from Stanford University told a reporter. "It is not possible to obtain a 100-percent result, certainly not from a dog."

Dr. McCulloch felt that Shing Ling had a normal dog's sense of smell. He didn't want people to think there was something extraordinary about her, so he and Dr. Broffman recruited other dogs. Three were Labrador Retrievers, two were Portuguese Water Dogs. None of the dogs had any prior experience using their noses for any such activity.

A Polish researcher, Professor Tadeusz Jezierski, Sc.D., of the Polish Academy of Sciences, traveled over from Poland to be lead investigator. The study was conducted over a period of four months in 2003; 12,295 separate scent trials were documented on videotape. Not only did the dogs perform exceptionally well, they did so consistently, distinguishing the breath of 55 lung cancer patients and 31 breast cancer patients from 83 healthy controls. If the dog detected cancer, he was trained to sit or lie down. For breath from lung cancer patients, Dr. McCulloch reported, the dogs sat correctly 564 times and incorrectly 10 times.

For the breath from healthy patients, they sat 4 times and did not sit 708 times. With adjustments made due to other factors, the researchers determined the accuracy rate at 99 percent.

The success rate of the clinic's study, as Dr. Donald Berry, from the M. D. Anderson Cancer Center in Houston, said, "is off the charts: there are no laboratory tests as good as this, not Pap tests, not diabetes tests, nothing."

Dr. McCulloch and Dr. Broffman wrote in their report:

"What is important about this study is that: (1) ordinary dogs, with no prior scent discrimination training, could be rapidly trained to identify lung and breast cancer patients by smelling samples of their breath, when compared to blank unused sample tubes; (2) dogs could accurately and reliably distinguish breath samples of lung and breast cancer patients from those of healthy controls; and (3) the dog's diagnostic performance was not affected by disease stage of cancer patients, age, smoking, or most recently eaten meal among either cancer patients or controls."

The results are astounding. Dogs with three weeks of training could detect cancer better than the latest CAT, PET, and MRI scanners, better than chest x-rays and sputum cytology. The breed of dog didn't matter. The stage of cancer didn't matter. The dogs picked it up, whether the patient was barely in Stage 1 or had progressed to invasive, metastasis Stage 4.

The results of the study were written up in the March 2006 issue of the journal *Integrative Cancer Therapies* titled "Diagnostic Accuracy of Canine Scent Detection of Lung and Breast Cancers in Exhaled Breath."

"We set out to see if cancer has a smell and if people with cancer have a different smell than people without cancer," Broffman said. "We were impressed with how well the dogs did."

A Japanese film crew came to make a documentary about Pine Street's cancer-detection dogs. As the filmmakers were setting up their cameras, getting ready to tape Shing Ling, the dog quietly went over to the cameraman and sat on his foot. He just thought she was being friendly, so he patted her on the head, and continued to work. Shing Ling stopped him by sitting on the cameraman's foot again, then looking pointedly at the trainer.

The trainer gave her a treat and told the doctors. It turned out his lungs had been x-rayed just before he left Japan, but the results were inconclusive. Dr. McCulloch urged him to see his doctor immediately upon his return.

"After that, people started getting worried if Shing Ling sat too close to them," Dr. McCulloch said.

The Pine Street Foundation was recently awarded a grant from the Congressionally Directed Medical Research Program for detecting ovarian cancer with the use of a dog's nose, in partnership with Touradj Solouki, Associate Professor of Chemistry at the University of Maine. Studies will be conducted using two of the most sensitive and sophisticated scent detection devices on the planet, a type of mass spectrometer and a dog's nose. The focus will be specifically on detecting ovarian cancer through analysis of exhaled breath, leading the way toward a truly non-invasive way to diagnose ovarian cancer. Five dogs will be used to discriminate between the epithelial ovarian cancer cells and healthy controls. Dogs will be trained to indicate the cancer patient samples by sitting directly in front of the cancer sample only, and sniffing but ignoring the samples from healthy controls.

⌒

IF DOGS CAN RECOGNIZE such odors, the implications for medicine could be enormous. Their noses might provide early detection that science cannot yet achieve.

Dr. Walker from FSU says there has been an unexpected, and heartbreaking, side to his research. Every time his studies make the headlines, he is flooded with phone calls, mostly from women, pleading with him to have his dog screen them for cancer. Dr. Walker has to explain that he can't do that as he's not a medical doctor. He also tells them that the testing is in an early phase. It is not an approved method. But he says the women don't care. Often, they have had cancer and gone through surgery, chemotherapy, and extensive treatment. They know that the rate of recidivism for cancer is extremely high. And they also know that current methods of detection are highly fallible. The women are terrified that the cancer might have come back. It's not that they don't trust their doctors. They do. It's just that they are willing to put their trust in dogs. Most of them have dogs of their own, so they know that a dog is always paying more attention to you than you do to yourself.

As I read the interviews with scientists about the canines detecting cancer, again and again the scientist would say, "The real importance of this study is to find out how the dog does it, and build a machine that can do it."

This was puzzling. The dogs were detecting cancer with an incredible record of success. They were discovering cancers that other methods of investigation had missed. Why then were scientists so eager to replace them with a machine?

Dr. Walker said the answer was easy: It's because they are dogs, and scientists are people who long for approval and acceptance in the world at large. The idea of dogs detecting cancer is only a joke to most doctors. Scientists like Dr. Walker, who design studies to prove the olfactory powers of dogs, are showered with derision. The general idea put to them is, "Come on, grow up and do some real science—quit messing around with dogs."

Dr. Wallace Sampson, editor of the *Scientific Review of Alternative Medicine* and a member of the board of directors of the National Council Against Health Fraud, was quoted in a newspaper article as saying, "I think it's this side of absurd. People's odors are such that any odor from a cancer cell would be overwhelmed by all of the smells given. Those smells would overwhelm the receptor. To say that cancer would suddenly be detectable by dogs is too far out for most scientists. It's implausible."

That sort of denial angers Dr. Walker, because, he says, "No one is saying, 'We will use only the dog to look for cancer.' Cancer is very complex. Right now, there are many methods used to detect it: blood work, biopsies, MRIs, second opinions. We're not saying, 'Let's replace X-rays, CT scans, fiber-optic scopes, mammograms, Pap smears, and other cancer screens with dogs.' We're saying, 'Here's an incredible tool which might help save your patients' lives.' Why laugh at it and turn it away?"

⌒

IF DOCTORS SCOFFED at the idea of cancer-sniffing dogs, there was another dog talent manifesting itself that had them positively roaring with laughter. Patients were starting to show up in doctors' offices with the outrageous claim that their dogs could predict their epileptic seizures. Their doctors tried to tell them that there was no technology invented yet that could do such a thing, so surely a dog couldn't do it. But these people, whose lives were ruled by the fear of having a seizure in public, wouldn't listen.

CHAPTER 13

IF YOU'RE SICK, I'LL LET YOU KNOW

FRAN ATKINS WAS HAVING a wonderful time in Philadelphia. She and her husband, Bob, had flown out from their home in the Pacific Northwest to visit Fran's brother and his wife. The siblings hadn't seen each other in years. And when they heard her brother had secured tickets to the Barbra Streisand concert, that was icing on the cake for the long-planned reunion.

Now, Fran stood near the ticket booths in Philadelphia's Wachovia Center, a cavernous indoor sports arena, while her husband asked about interpreters for people with hearing disabilities. Her young service dog, Hotei, a black-and-white Akita, stood by her side.

Fran had lost hearing in her left ear when she was twelve years old, and hearing in her right ear went in and out, like static on a radio. Fran was one of the many lucky people who had benefited from Bonnie Bergin's invention, back in 1975, of the service dog. For the past fourteen years, she'd been accompanied by a hearing dog who signaled her when alarms went off, telephones rang, or a car honked at her as she crossed the street.

Hotei had done marvelously on this trip so far. He learned best when he watched how Tedi, her six-year-old brown-and-white Akita, handled new things. On this trip, Hotei had been through the bustling Portland, Oregon, airport, undressed from his service-dog harness by the Department of Homeland Security, flown for the first time at Fran's feet in a plane, and accompanied her to the Liberty Bell and Valley Forge National Historic Park, where tourists had swarmed the two dogs. Hotei was getting a lot of good training.

Before coming to the Streisand concert, they had arranged in advance for interpreters to sit with Fran so she'd know what was going on.

However, Fran had been thinking to herself that Hotei was behaving a little unusually tonight. He'd stopped paying attention to the people in the crowds, and failed to acknowledge some children they'd met earlier. He'd refused to lie down at dinner, insisting on sitting by her side. Suddenly, he reared up and put his paws against Fran's belly, pinning her to the wall. Panic raced through her and she called out to Bob. Now she knew what was wrong with Hotei: He was alerting her that she was about to have a seizure.

Before Bob could reach her, Fran's body went limp and slipped to the floor. Spasms jerked her muscles, pulling her arms up and down. She began to vomit. Fran never knew when her seizures would hit, and when they did, she didn't know if they would be brief or extended ones, like this.

Fran recalled the awful event as she spoke to me from her home in Everett, Washington. She explained that the seizures were brought on by her Ménière's Disease, which is a compilation of symptoms: vertigo, tinnitus, hearing loss, and a sensation of pressure in the ears. As she speaks, Hotei lies in the corner of her living room, his ears alert, his dark brown eyes on Fran. Tedi, the older Akita, snoozes on the couch.

Fran looks comfortable and at peace with her two service dogs near her. She has explained these painful details many times before. She is a small woman with a slight build, so the average Akita, which weighs around one hundred pounds, looks even bigger standing next to her.

"I got Bear fourteen years ago, when my sister-in-law decided it was time I stopped cowering in my house and got a hearing dog. Her shepherd got together with an Akita in the backyard, and she gave me one of the puppies."

Bear died at age thirteen. His photos are kept prominently on Fran's website. He was a black-masked fawn dog, with alert ears and far-seeing eyes. His watchful attitude in his photos gives the impression that he knew he was Fran's guardian.

"We started Bear's training when he was eight weeks old. My husband and my friends helped me. We enrolled in Paws-Abilities, a training program in the greater Seattle area. Their focus is mainly on obedience and agility dog training, but every Saturday afternoon, they have a class for teaching service dogs."

Fran had not been looking for an alert dog. She did not know there was such a thing. The idea that your dog could alert you that a seizure was coming seemed to good to be true.

"Bear was just over a year old when he started showing signs of alerting me to my particular disorder. At first, I didn't understand what he was doing. I didn't know why he would act so strangely. Then one day, he wouldn't leave me alone. He followed me everywhere, even into the bathroom. He lay down on the bathroom floor. He was staring at me, like he was pleading with me, but I couldn't understand what he wanted. I lay down on the bed and he put his head on my stomach. Later on that evening I ended up in the emergency room because I was hemorrhaging."

Fran realized that Bear had known she was sick and was trying to let her know.

"After that, we paid attention to all the things he was doing, like touching me for no reason. All of a sudden, he'd be very, very attentive. He'd get up and put his head on my lap. Shortly after, I would have an attack. It was obvious Bear knew these attacks were coming and wanted to warn me." Nothing could be done to prevent Fran's attacks, but now she knew they were coming and could at least make sure she was not in a dangerous place or position when they struck.

At the training class, Bear's alerting behavior made him something of a celebrity. "There were people with MS and epilepsy and other kinds of seizure disorders. One time, Bear got up and walked to a woman with MS who was in a wheelchair. He'd never noticed her before. This time, he put his head on her lap. I looked at her and I looked at Dana, one of the owners of Paws-Abilities, and said: 'She's going to have a seizure. That's what he does to me when I get sick.'

"They believed me because they'd seen Bear alert me before. Within ten minutes she had a seizure."

Paws-Abilities trainer Dana Babb confirms Fran's account. She remembers teaching Fran to train Bear as what she refers to as a 'signal dog' because of her hearing problems. That was Bear's first duty, and he was very good at it. Not long after he started training, he saved Fran from a smoky fire. "One night, my husband was at work, and I was asleep. The next thing I know, Bear is on top of the bed, grabbing my hand. He was trying to pull me off the bed. I didn't want to go. I said, 'Go away.' But he was insistent. He dragged me and made me follow him to the front door and go out. It turned out the smoke alarm was going off, and I never heard it. He got me out of the house."

The whole family experienced more peace than they'd known in a long time. No one had to be with Fran every minute anymore, because Bear was there, and he was better at helping her than they were. "If my husband and I get separated at a store, we whistle to find each other. Bear would take me to where the whistle was coming from."

Dana Babb knew that Bear understood his job as a signal, or hearing, dog. But she says: "Bear was one of the first dogs to show me that a service dog could also be an alert dog. Before that, I hadn't heard much about it. Back then, the idea sounded kind of far-fetched. How the heck is the dog going to figure out you're going to have a seizure?"

Fran and Dana both researched alert dogs on their own. There was very little literature on the subject. But in recent years, medical evidence in support of seizure-alert dogs is slowly piling up. A study by researchers at the School of Health Policy and Practice at the University of East Anglia reported in the January 1999 and January 2001 issues of *Seizure* magazine confirmed that dogs who had been trained to respond to their owners' seizures with assistance sometimes developed "the ability to predict and react in advance of an oncoming seizure."

A 1998 University of Florida study surveyed epileptics who owned dogs. Sixty-three patients completed a questionnaire. Twenty-nine owned dogs. Nine reported that their dogs responded to a seizure by remaining close to them, either standing or lying alongside them, sometimes licking their face or hands during and immediately after the seizure. Of the nine dogs, three were reported to also alert their human to an impending seizure.

The study indicated that the dog was more likely to alert to a person with a migraine headache or certain types of "auras" before their seizures. The effectiveness of the seizure-alerting dog depended greatly on the ability of the human to recognize and respond to the dog's behavior.

A British charity, Support Dogs, reported that they were able to train dogs "to recognize specific changes preceding a seizure and give an overt signal enabling the dog to warn his/her owner." The trainers noted that the dogs were completely accurate in their predictions. An unexpected but interesting side note was that in each case the owners started to have fewer seizures. Since stress can increase the frequency of seizures and it has been shown in numerous studies that dogs lower stress, perhaps there is no mystery to this finding.

One thing some of the researchers noticed was that the alert dogs took their jobs very seriously. If they were separated from their owner, they showed signs of stress and anxiety until they could be next to the owner again. They wanted to do the job.

In the *British Medical Journal*, Dr. Gareth Williams and his associates from the Liverpool University Hospital reported on three case histories in which a pet dog sensed an imminent hypoglycemic shock in their owner and warned them ahead of time to take proper treatment.

In the first case, a sixty-six-year-old woman with type 2 diabetes had been experiencing frequent episodes of excessive sweating, general weakness, anxiety, and irritability. These attacks would occur in the evening. Over the course of a year, she found her nine-year-old mixed breed dog, Candy, would jump up and run out of the room and hide when an episode was about to occur. She came back only when the patient took carbohydrates to stabilize her condition. The dog started to act this way well before she was aware of her symptoms.

The second case described a similar 'early warning' ability of another pet dog, a seven-year-old mixed breed called Susie who would nudge her owner, a forty-seven-year-old woman. Susie sensed the impending hypoglycemic episode, even when her owner was asleep. She would wake her up, at which point the woman would eat and her symptoms would recede.

And in the third case, the same type of alarm was raised by a three-year-old Golden Retriever, Natt, who sensed the coming of an episode and alerted his owner by pacing up and down and putting his head on her lap. At nights, he would bark and paw against her bedroom door.

The professors who wrote the article were so impressed with the ability of these dogs that they honored them by including their names as co-authors of the paper.

How dogs detect an oncoming seizure in a human remains a mystery. Some trainers and researchers think they detect subtle changes in their owner's behavior or movements. Some think they can sense the "aura" that precedes a seizure. Or maybe they are aware that the brain waves of a person about to seizure are substantially different from normal. But most researchers are arriving at the opinion that what is at work here is the dog's incredible power of scent. There are as yet no scientific studies to prove this, because no doctor or medical machine is sensitive enough to be able to detect a change of scent. But Dr. Walker, of the Sensory Research Institute, documented that the dogs he used to sniff out cancer cells could smell a chemical in a few parts per trillion. He says it seems logical to him that a dog could detect a change in a human's smell. "I would be surprised if they couldn't do it."

OVER THE YEARS, Bear and Fran grew extremely close. His alerting behavior gave Fran the confidence to resume her daily life. When Bear was seven, he started to get arthritis in his back. Fran realized she would need another dog so Bear could retire. She had a friend who owned an Akita, and she'd been surprised to discover that when she visited her friend's home, the untrained Akita would come over and alert to her seizure, the same way Bear did.

Since Bear was half Akita, Fran started to think that his breed was particularly sensitive to her condition. Akitas are striking and impressive creatures, about 27 inches tall, with strong, thick bones and a weight of approximately one hundred pounds when fully grown. They have large, bear-like heads with erect, triangular ears, thick coats, and tight cat feet. Their tails curl over the top of their backs in a graceful sweep; they have an attitude of nobility. In their early history in Japan, only shoguns could own Akitas. They were the dog of royalty, not the common man. Akitas also exhibit an air of being relaxed and calm and in control, which is very comforting to people who don't feel that way.

Fran decided a purebred Akita was exactly what she needed. But how to know if the new puppy would have the same ability that Bear did?

"With my particular condition, there are things I have to avoid because they might trigger an attack. When we were going to the home of the breeder, I did all the things I wasn't supposed to do, like have a lot of salt and eat a tomato.

"The breeder, Brenda, let one Akita out. He came and kissed me, then ran to play with my husband. Dogs love my husband.

"The next Akita did the same thing.

"The third one came over to me, crawled into my lap and licked my face. She did that funny little circle that they do and lay down in my lap so I couldn't get up. Shortly after that, I started feeling an attack. So I knew she was the Akita for me."

Tedi's coloring was totally different from Bear's beige-fawn. She was a pinto, mostly white with patches of brown and a black head. She was truly striking.

Fran had not trained Bear to alert her. It was something he had decided to do on his own. So she didn't know how to train a new puppy. But Bear took over in an amazing way. He trained the puppy. When it was time to alert Fran, he ran over to her and put his paw on her lap. The puppy followed him and did the same thing, and Fran gave both dogs a treat.

"The first time Bear alerted to me with Tedi around, Tedi gave me the funniest look. It was like she was saying, I know something's wrong. I don't know what it is. She sat by my side while Bear had his head in my lap. I'd praise her and give her a treat when she came with Bear to alert me. And she just learned how to do it.

"Then when Bear got ill and couldn't alert anymore, Tedi would look at him as if saying, 'Well, are you going to do your job?' And if Bear didn't get up off the couch, she would go do the job.

"Tedi is funny because she is much more aggressive about alerting me than the males have been. One time, I was at work, and I started going down the stairs. Suddenly, she slammed into me and forced me against the wall. She wouldn't let me go up. She wouldn't let me go down. I had to sit down and stay right where I was. She leaned against me to keep me there.

"Another time, I was at my friend Michael's house, looking at all the ribbons he won at dog shows. Tedi was in a down-stay command in the corner. Suddenly she raced over to me and reared up and put her head on my shoulder. I said, 'Uh-oh.' Within fifteen minutes I was really, really sick. I had one of the most severe vertigo attacks I'd ever had."

"When you suffer from vertigo, you lose your balance and it's easy to fall. When my dogs alert me, I get myself into a position where I can't fall.

"She has different levels. If it's going to be a mild attack, She'll lightly touch me. She nudges me. If it's going to be a bad attack, she puts all her weight into it.

"My friend Selma didn't believe me until she saw Tedi do this. She just said, Oh, sure. She thought I was imagining it. One day I was at her place and we were going out to shop. Selma was going to drive. I went to open the car door, and Tedi turned around and went back and sat at the front door. She would not get in that car. She wouldn't let me put her in. My friend thought that was hilarious. She said, your dog knows you better than you do! When Tedi saw Selma get into the driver's seat, then she got in the car. She made sure I wasn't driving.

"Shortly after that, I had an attack. She was alerting me."

With Tedi approaching age six, Fran decided to look for her third service dog. She wanted only another purebred Akita. She did the same thing she had done to pick out Tedi, making herself purposefully sick to see which puppy was concerned and came over.

Fran said, "Two puppies came to me, but one was sold. The other was Hotei." Hotei was a heavily black-marked pinto, very distinct from Tedi's mostly white coloring. He had a longish coat, unusual for an Akita.

Again, Fran worried about Hotei having the skill to alert. She wished she could fake a seizure, to see if he would alert to it, but that's not possible. Certain chemicals are released into the bloodstream when a person has a seizure, and medical science doesn't know what they are or how to imitate them.

"Hotei watched Tedi and did everything she did. The first time she alerted, he came over, too, and I gave them both a treat. After that, I'd see Hotei stick his head up and run over to me. He was trying to alert me first and get the biggest treat!

"Within the first few months he was with me, Hotei did an alert that my first dog had never done. I was asleep, and having an attack in my sleep. Next thing I know, I have this puppy Akita on top of me. He jumped on the bed and woke me up."

Fran says Hotei usually nudges her very gently when he alerts. But she knows that he means, 'Okay, something is wrong, pay attention.'"

Fran's hobby is the craft of egg decorating. Having an alert dog has meant she is able to attend craft shows, even ones far from her home. "This past weekend, I was at an egg show, decorating my egg. All of a sudden, Hotei comes out of his down-stay and runs over and starts nudging my hand. I really wanted to stay and work on that egg. The instructor owns Rottweilers and she said to me: 'Hey! Pay attention to your dog. He's telling you something.' I said, 'Yeah, okay,' and packed up the egg and went and found a sofa to lie on while I got sick. About ten minutes later, I got very dizzy and nauseous. It was a really mild attack and lasted about half an hour.

"As I get older, my attacks are getting worse. But my dogs are getting better! Bear used to give me five or ten minutes' warning. Tedi gave me fifteen or twenty. Now, Hotei lets me know a whole half hour ahead of time."

Paws-Abilities trainer Dana Babb said that fourteen years ago, when Bear started to alert, "the idea was treated with much skepticism. Bear is one of the dogs who taught me that alert dogs really did exist. These dogs not only can, and do, alert to seizures, they alert to blood-sugar changes for their diabetic owners, and we have taught several to alert their owners to migraines."

Most trainers think it's the luck of the draw; your dog trains himself to alert, or he doesn't.* There's nothing you can do to teach him. Interestingly, Dana is one of the few dog trainers who believe that a dog can be taught to alert. "You have to have the right dog. If someone brings me a puppy who's all about chasing sticks and tennis balls and is not interested in their owner unless he has a tennis ball in his hand, this dog is probably not going to

---

* The Epilepsy Foundation has heard a lot about alert dogs over the years. Articles about them have been published in the foundation's magazine and on its Web site. So the staff there knows that the ability to alert is still rare. They are concerned that unscrupulous dog trainers might take advantage of a person with the desperate hope that a dog will alert them. In a press statement, the foundation said that "since there is currently no way of knowing what kind of training is needed to develop these skills in dogs, nor even whether it is possible to do so, the Epilepsy Foundation suggests that people should be cautious about purchasing 'seizure dogs.'"

be a good seizure alert dog, and probably not even a good service dog. The dogs have to care about their humans. You need the kind of dog that would like to be next to you all the time and notices when you don't feel well."

Dana said that people are beginning to acknowledge that there are dogs who can alert their owners to seizures. "One of my clients was at her neurologist's office for an appointment, and the doctor witnessed her Standard Poodle stand up and alert her. Shortly after, she had a seizure. The doctor was stunned."

Another of her clients' dogs, a Shetland Sheepdog called Toby, was with his owner at a banquet when he suddenly started to become agitated. He wasn't trying to alert her, he was walking to the end of his leash and looking at another table. She let him loose and he immediately went up to a fifty-year-old-man and put his paw on his leg. She told the man, "That's how he alerts me that I'm going to have a seizure."

The people at the dinner table got a good laugh out of it. The man said he was in good health and not in danger of seizure. They looked on it as an example of how crazy some people are about their dogs.

But later that night, the man was at home when he had a heart attack and died.

Dana said: "That Sheltie had to be retired because he was so sensitive. The owner would be in the emergency room and he would be trying to go around and alert all these people that they were sick. It made him frustrated and anxious if people wouldn't pay attention."

I asked what could be done in advance if a dog alerted his owner that a migraine was coming. "We teach them to bring the medicine. The person is sitting there feeling fine, but if the dog brings the bottle of pills over, they take one right away. It can sometimes prevent the migraine."

I tried to imagine what it would be like to have your dog

show up with a bottle of pills and a look in his eyes that said, "You better take these."

Dana said she had trained all breeds of dogs as service dogs and alert dogs, and there was no one best breed. Individuals in every breed seemed able to do it.

But Fran Atkins is sticking with her favorite. "I've been around other types of dogs, but to me, I think, the Akita is the most sensitive of all of them."

Fran wrote a memoriam to Bear, which stays up on her Web site: "You were my life line to the outside world. I started hiking again because of you. We would go to the beach because you were by my side. You gave me back my confidence to be out in public with only you by my side. You were my ears when I couldn't hear. You were my guide. You gave me back my life."

SANDY BARNETT HAS LIVED in the dry climate of Phoenix, Arizona, for only a few years. But she has lived with seizures for most of her life. She's had seven brain surgeries to remove an oligodendroglioma tumor that keeps growing back in her left temporal lobe. A meningioma tumor hides behind it. Her surgeons have found it impossible to remove all of the tumors in her brain. The tumors have made her an epileptic subject to many different kinds of seizures, including grand mal and petit mal.

A seizure hits without warning. Sandy says, "I only know a seizure is on the way when I'm already having it."

Seizures are so disruptive to her life that she had to quit her job as an assistant to the managers of Wendy's restaurants. For many years, she was afraid to go anywhere on her own. One day, at her surgeon's office, she was fascinated to see a woman with a Shih Tzu on her lap whom the woman claimed was a service dog. "I was amazed because I thought service dogs were only big ones, like Labrador Retrievers and German Shepherds. Then I found out that she had a seizure disorder, and the dog was an alert dog."

The woman's husband had been taken to a treatment room in the back of the office, while she and Sandy sat up front in the waiting room. Suddenly, the Shih Tzu started to bark. The nurse thought he was alerting to a seizure and rushed the woman into the back. But it wasn't a seizure. In the treatment room, they found that her husband, who had Parkinson's Disease, had collapsed on the floor.

"The dog was alerting to the husband, and he wasn't even in the same room," Sandy says.

That day, the surgeon told Sandy, "I want you to get a service dog."

"We couldn't have a dog where we lived because there was a 'No Pets' rule. My surgeon told me about the law; if I got a service dog, they had to let him live with me. They had no choice. The doctor thought a service dog would help me have some freedom.

"I took my time looking around for a dog. I knew that not every dog would be able to alert. I had to find the right one. I looked at Rat Terriers and Shih Tzus and Pomeranians and Poodles. I found some that were grown dogs and some that were puppies. I just didn't go out and pick a dog. You have to let the dog pick you. He has to choose to be bound to you. It doesn't matter the breed. It's how he reacts to you.

"After five months, I found a photo of a black-and-tan Chihuahua on the Arizona Chihuahua rescue site. He was eight and a half pounds. When I saw him, I felt I just had to meet him. The woman who runs rescue brought him over. She said she'd taken him to adoption fairs for three weeks in a row and was surprised that no one wanted him. But he was very sensitive and reserved. He didn't jump up to see everybody.

"She handed him to me and we got attached right away. I put him down beside me, and he climbed right back up in my lap. She went out to her car to get his adoption papers, and when she came back I said, 'He's the one.'

"I failed to ask, 'Do they bark much?' That's the one thing I'd change about the dear boy."

Little Ben was a year old. Sandy started him in basic obedience classes, where, she said, "He was the littlest and the loudest."

Five months after the arrival of Little Ben, Sandy had some kind of disturbance while she was sleeping. Suddenly she felt a little muzzle poking her arm and trying to lift it up. "I woke up, and his face was three inches from my face. He stayed right there until he saw that I was okay. Then he crawled back under the covers.

"I was very emotional after that. I kept crying and crying and thanking the Lord. It was too wonderful to believe, that this little dog would react like that to my seizures.

"The next time, he jumped in my lap and looked in my face very urgently. Then he started pawing me. Then I understood. He was right, I had a seizure.

"Another time, I was in the bathtub, and he was sleeping in his little bed beside me. All of a sudden he was jumping up and down, trying to put his feet on the edge and get to my shoulder. He was alerting to the aura. I knew I had to get out of there because I was going to have a seizure.

"They don't know if the dog can sense the brain waves, or it's a chemical that gets into my blood that they smell. I don't have to worry now about having a seizure, because I know this little guy is going to alert me. Before, I was afraid to go out, but now, I go everywhere. He travels in a stroller or a belly pouch.

"I've prayed many times and gave thanks for this miracle. It was incredible. It gave me such peace. And such confidence. Now I know that whenever he is with me, I'm safe. I'm not going to be knocked out, hurt myself, and fall down in a strange place. He won't let that happen. This little guy has been such an asset to me and such an asset to the family. We all feel safer because of him.

"That's a pretty good deal to get in only 8-and-a-half pounds."

⌒

WHEN I STARTED THIS RESEARCH, I had been told again and again that it was not possible to train a seizure alert dog. Such dogs only arose spontaneously. They trained themselves. They were highly unusual dogs with close attachments to their sick owners. This is still true. Most of these dogs do arise spontaneously. But as this field evolves, some trainers say that they have figured out how to train alert dogs. It seems to have a lot to do with training the dog to *respond* to the seizure by bringing medication, or a phone, or a purse, or alerting another human; staying close while the seizure lasts; licking the hands and cheeks to try to bring the person back to consciousness. Once he reliably does all these things, some dogs transition themselves to beginning these behaviors before the seizure starts. If the human notices, he has time to take seizure-blocking medication, or lie down so he won't fall and be hurt.

It was also thought that it would not be possible to pick out which dog or puppy would be accurately able to alert. And yet, several of the people I interviewed had picked out a dog who could alert them. Their ability to do that probably has more to do with the intuition that Malcolm Gladwell describes in his book, Blink, than conscious knowledge of what traits can be physically or intellectually perceived in a good alert dog. They were doing what Gladwell calls "thin slicing," judging by signals so small that they are not consciously aware of them.

⌐⊃

JENNIFER ARNOLD OF GEORGIA has taken the matter a step further. She runs Canine Assistants, a service dog organization in Alpharetta, just north of Atlanta. The organization has a sort of sub-specialty in alert dogs. She is walking on the leading edge in alert dog training.

Jennifer Arnold is a bright presence, with dark hair and a strong smile that makes it easy to believe that she put together this top-flight service dog academy by herself. "87.2 percent of the dogs we place with people with epilepsy or seizure disorders learn to alert with in the first year of placement," she says.

That's an amazing figure. She hastens to add that they do not guarantee a dog who will alert. But it has worked out that way 87.2 percent of the time.

"My lifelong goal is to learn to what stimuli the dogs are responding," Jennifer said on a summer afternoon at her head quarters, an 18-acre facility. "I don't have to be able to smell it. I just have to be able to reproduce it."

She says she's pretty sure now that it's a smell that gets the dogs' attention. "I used to think it was a combination of an electrical field change and odor, but now I think its just smell."

Her opinion was formed when a young man with a Canine Assistants dog was hospitalized at Louisiana State University in the epilepsy-monitoring unit. He was hooked up to EEG monitors that continuously recorded his brain waves. A video camera was focused on him. Jennifer says, "Not just once, but twice, you see the dog get upset and anticipate the seizure. This dog had already developed, during camp, the ability to anticipate onset. Initially, the dog gets restless and whines and paces. A minute before the seizure actually hits, the dog jumps up on the bed and starts nuzzling him on the hand. That's the way she's always alerted. The interesting thing—on the monitor, there is absolutely no change in the young man's brainwaves until the actual seizure starts. That dumped my enthusiasm for the theory of electrical change because it would be unlikely that the monitor would not detect an electrical impulse."

How is it possible for Canine Assistants to claim such a high rate of success, when so many service dog handlers say confidently that an alert dog cannot be trained? The dogs are bred on site, and they are the same breeds most often used; the Labrador Retriever, Golden Retriever, and crosses between the two.

But these dogs don't go out to spend the first year with families. Their training starts the third day after they are born, with a protocol of five neuromotor stimulations. These continue through day sixteen. Jennifer says, "It's made an incredible difference. The dogs are much more stable. They can handle a lot more stress and they are flexible in situations."

Dams leave their puppies when they are four weeks old, which is young. Most other kennels don't wean puppies until they are six or even eight weeks old. The trainers take over the maternal duties of comforting, teaching and leading the puppies. By the time they are eight weeks old, the puppies have been introduced to thirty-seven commands. Jennifer says that they are proficient in doing ten to twelve of the commands on cue. An eight-week-old puppy is what you see in the pet shop, wagging his tail and playing with a toy. It is very much a baby.

But at eight weeks, Canine Assistants puppies are good at heeling, shaking hands, and waiting when told. They know "sit," "down," "roll over," and "settle." Jennifer says, "Because the dogs learn so quickly so young, it's really critical to have them in the hands of professionals during that time. Our dogs stay with us through the entire process. They have volunteers who take them out for weekend home visits. Multiple times, they'll go home for a home visit for a couple of weeks. But their education comes first."

At eight months, while most other service dogs are living with a family, the Canine Assistants know all ninety-two of the service dog commands. They can open doors, fetch medicine bottles, pick up clothing and pull a wheelchair. Most of the Canine Assistants' dogs graduate between eighteen months and two years of age.

That's considered young by most organizations. But Jennifer Arnold has a very strong philosophy about age. "You may have a lot more puppy behaviors to contend with if you place the dog when he's under two years of age," she says. "But I feel very strongly that if you can get the dog to the recipient before maturation has set in, they will have a stronger bond. If you get a dog when he's grown up, he can grow to love you dearly. But when you've had them for any part of the immaturity phase, it almost seems like a different kind of bond."

Jennifer says it's also crucial to match the dog's personality to recipient's. "Most dogs choose their own people," she says. "We let them. It's really interesting how the dogs seem to have a handle on the whole thing."

The more sensitive dogs are directed towards the people with seizure disorders. Jennifer says, "It's a seizure *response* dog. I don't want to use that word, 'alert.' Because we can't guarantee that. During training camp, we determine what is the most appropriate way for the dog to respond to a seizure."

Some of the dogs wear big signs that say, "If my partner has a seizure, please look in my pouch." Some dogs are taught to go for help. Some dogs learn to stay beside the person and watch over them. The trainers teach the family to encourage the dog to respond with them to the person having the seizure.

"We have a dog who literally within three days learned that when her person seizures, she gets the phone, brings it to her, gets her medicine bag, bring it to her, gets water out of the refrigerator, brings it to her, so that when she regains consciousness she can call for help and take her pills."

Jennifer says that it is now becoming common for their dogs to start alerting to seizures during the two-week training camp.

"At one training camp, the first morning, a little boy, seven years old from San Diego, California, came into the room. There was a sweet young Golden Retriever in one of the crates. She was always very quiet. Never made any trouble. All of a sudden, the dog went berserk. I didn't know what was going on with her. It was startling the way she was behaving. I got her out of the crate, and she literally pulled away from me, ran to this little boy, grabbed his shirt, and started trying to pull him out of his wheelchair. I knew as soon as she started pawing him that we needed to get him on a mat on the floor. Two minutes later, he had a grand mal seizure.

"This dog, Tess, had never met anyone with a seizure. She had never, ever seen a seizure before. I can absolutely tell you that for a fact."

How is it possible that a dog who never saw a seizure could recognize one? "I think it's a very bad smell. It must be wicked. They recognize that it hurts their person. I'm wondering about the other dogs. I've always wanted to tour around and sit with the dogs who people say their dog does not anticipate onset because I wonder if they are getting it, but the family is missing the cue."

Jennifer tells me that the little boy died just last week, after five years with Tess. How does a dog react when their partner dies? "Tess is just a basket case. We've had that happen many times. It's almost worse than the other way around. The dogs grieve so desperately that several times they've been unwilling to eat and had to be put on IVs. This is their mate, and they mated for life."

Does the family keep the dog? "Oh, you better believe it. In the industry, it's been somewhat controversial. To me, that's not a controversy. The dog stays. I'm not letting you lose your baby and your baby's dog at the same time. That's just cruel. The dogs are more than robotic assistants. I think they become family members."

Why did Jennifer decide to work with alert dogs?

"Epilepsy sucks. Sorry to put it that way. Have you ever known anybody who has seizures? I didn't until we got into this business, and it's the worse thing I've ever seen. I cannot imagine walking around every single day wondering when the ax is going to fall. Where are you going to be? Are you going to wet your pants in front of everybody in your class? The kids say, 'I'm not going to school. I'm not going to let people see me like this again.'" Having a dog makes the situation totally different, Jennifer says. The dogs alert 20 to 40 minutes before the seizure, giving the child time to call the nurse and prepare.

Jennifer says she's been amazed that the dogs who alert always want their people on the ground. "Always. They will literally pull them off the couch. They don't even want them on the bed. They want them flat on the floor. And it is very much as if they instinctively recognize what's going to happen, and that the person is going to fall."

After seventeen years of training service dogs, Jennifer sometimes asks herself why dogs continue to work so hard for us. "It's a mystery," she says. "In my opinion, it's the only thing that points to any lack of intelligence in a dog. I think it's rather that they are so kind and so committed to people. And it's so much a part of their genetics. We have an obligation to be nicer to them than we have up to now."

CHAPTER 14

AN ARMY OF TWO

ARMY SGT. FIRST CLASS Russell Joyce and his Special Forces unit had a dangerous assignment at the start of the U.S.-led invasion of Iraq, Operation Iraqi Freedom. Together, they were airdropped near Mosul, Iraq's third largest city, 225 miles northwest of Baghdad, as part of the effort to topple the country's leader, Saddam Hussein. Sunni Arabs of Saddam's Ba'ath party largely controlled the city, but its two million people included Arabs, Kurds, Armenians, Assyrians, and Turkmans. Hussein had viciously persecuted the Kurds to try to get them to leave the city. So when Sergeant Joyce's Special Forces unit, Third Group, Alpha Company, Third Battalion, showed up, the Kurdish *peshmerga** were happy to assist them.

The area around Mosul has been inhabited continuously for 2,000 years. It has seen many conflicts and invasions.

---

* *peshmerga*—name for Kurdish fighting forces. Translated to English as "those who face death."

Some people still call it by the ancient name, *Nineveh*. Now it was the scene of intense fighting between Hussein's troops and the American soldiers.

Sergeant Joyce's unit were a close, tightly knit group, which had been together during "Operation Enduring Freedom" in Afghanistan, the U.S. response to 9/11. Sergeant Joyce was the newest member to this unit. The others had seen lots of action together, and faced with the security problems in Mosul, they told the sergeant that they needed the extra protection a trained Military Working Dog could provide. The team previously had used dogs for sentry (guard) duties while stationed in Afghanistan; the dogs had proven to be a highly useful deterrent against people entering the compound.

This was in the early days of the invasion of Iraq, so that there was no possibility of receiving an official MWD from the States. But Special Forces units are trained to improvise for what they need on the battlefield. So when a local Kurdish leader named Kordo asked what Sergeant Joyce needed, he told them to bring him a police dog. He didn't think there was any possibility the Kurds could come up with one. Dogs are considered *haram* (forbidden), and religious law prohibits Muslims from touching them.

He found the stories his men told about the MWD they'd had in Afghanistan hard to believe. They said the dog guarded camp, alerted them to the presence of intruders, ran point on patrol, and steered them away from stepping on explosive metal devices. He thought his unit really wanted a dog merely as a distraction and a pet.

Yet Kordo told Sergeant Joyce he knew of two dogs. One was a German Shepherd, the other a Rottweiler. These dogs supposedly had worked with the Iraqi police, and Kordo thought one of them may suit their needs. Stateside, Sergeant Joyce's pet of choice had been a Doberman Pinscher. His observation of Rottweilers was that they could be hard to handle at times. So he asked for the shepherd.

About two weeks later, the Kurdish Maslawi[*] entered their camp, with two men holding a tightly wrapped carpet. The men unrolled the carpet, and, to the soldiers' shock, out popped what looked to be a German Shepherd.

The average American-raised German Shepherd weighs 75–80 pounds; this dog who emerged from the carpet, obviously a pure-bred, weighed only half that, about 36 pounds. The Kurds had found him chained up in one of the many police stations that Saddam Hussein's forces had abandoned. His ribs and bone structure stood out clearly because he'd obviously been starving for many days, and showed signs of abuse: his face and front legs were scarred from repeated beatings and upon further inspection, they found that his mouth was missing his two lower canine teeth.

Sergeant Joyce asked Kordo if the dog even had a name. "Tariq Aziz," the response, made the Americans chuckle because "Tariq Aziz" was also the name of the Hussein's deputy prime minister (1979–2003), who was the de facto ruler who terrified the Iraqis. As Hussein's right-hand man, he was one of the most wanted men in Iraq after the fall of Baghdad; his face became clearly displayed on one of those playing cards that announced a reward for his capture. One soldier suggested his name should be "Terror," short for "Terrified."

On the dog's first night in the compound, he didn't bark or make any sound at all. He cowered in the shadows, seemingly afraid that this new bunch of uniformed men would kick and beat him, as had happened many times before.

Some men in the unit suggested to Sergeant Joyce that he turn the dog loose. Terror looked nothing like the MWD they had in mind. They thought a scared animal like this would never be able

---

[*] Maslawi–a person who lives in Mosul.

to do sentry duty. The only reason Sergeant Joyce didn't take their advice was because he wanted to maintain the good relationship with the Kurds, and he knew they had worked hard to get him this dog. "Let's give him a chance," he told the men. "We can always give him away later."

Sergeant Joyce was secretly sorry he had not tried harder to talk the team out of requesting the dog. It was pretty clear that in this shape, the dog would not be a deterrent to anyone. Not only was he too thin and scared, he had no energy. The first day, he collapsed in a heap. "He literally didn't move for a day," Sergeant Joyce said.

The first problem was finding something to feed him. With obviously no dog food in Iraq, dogs ate scraps from meals or whatever they could find. Sergeant Joyce fed Terror mutton, fried chicken, and rice out of his hand. He fed the dog whatever he was eating, right from his own plate. And Terror was grateful, relaxing a little in Sergeant Joyce's company.

But the second night was also a disaster. When darkness fell, Terror began to bark, and kept it up through the entire night. The sentry determined that a pack of stray dogs was just outside the fence, foraging through garbage for scraps of food, and that was what Terror was carrying on about. The men couldn't sleep. In the morning, they were once again in favor of getting rid of the dog. But Sergeant Joyce still insisted on giving him a chance.

As things turned out, it was a good decision. Sergeant Joyce had taken his Doberman Pinschers to obedience school, and he was familiar with a positive, reward-based method of training. But he didn't know anything about military training of K-9s. He was also a little disgruntled that despite being the one who did not initially want the dog, he was now the one responsible for taking care of and training him. With some food in his belly, Terror started to learn what was asked of him very quickly. He learned basic commands such as heel, sit, and stay.

After just a few nights with his new American friends, Sergeant Joyce noticed Terror snap his head to attention and stare out into the night, beyond the fence. Sergeant Joyce couldn't see anything, but he decided to encourage the dog, patting him and telling him "Good!" Thus encouraged, Terror began to bark loudly. Looking in the same direction, Sergeant Joyce saw several men sprint out of their hiding places. They were insurgents, and they'd been waiting for the right moment to get a shot at the Americans. But with a dog on the scene, they decided it wasn't worth it. They were extremely fearful of dogs. Just the thought that the dog might run after and bite them was enough to send them fleeing from the compound.

Sergeant Joyce looked down at Terror in amazement and patted his head. "You might have just saved my life," he said. In that moment the role of the war dog as a deterrent was very clear to him.

Terror continued to learn his job at an amazing pace. In only two weeks he could correctly walk patrol, staying on Sergeant Joyce's left, stopping when he stopped, looking in the direction he pointed. When Sergeant Joyce had to leave on patrols, friends who were in the rear would help take care of him, following Sergeant Joyce's directions to echo the commands he used so that the dog would begin to understand English.

Encouraged by Sergeant Joyce, Terror barked ferociously whenever he scented someone suspicious moving near the compound.

One night as they walked along, Terror spotted someone in the compound and tore loose from Sergeant Joyce's hands. It was a Kurdish soldier, someone friendly to the Americans, but he was an Iraqi, and Terror knew the difference between Americans and everyone else. He chased the man over a fence, tearing off his pants.

One of the best things about that incident was that everyone in the unit saw it. They were impressed.

Terror lived through two shooting incidents. One of the men joked that the Shepherd, because he was rescued and fed by Special Forces, and came under fire twice without being hit, ought to have his name changed to "Lucky." That hit a chord. Sergeant Joyce wasn't comfortable calling this dog "Terror" anymore. No one on the team came up with any suggestions, so Sergeant Joyce joked that he would change it to something his two little girls would like. "Like what?" one soldier asked.

Sergeant Joyce thought about Samantha and Elise and their lovely little girl bedrooms back home, with billowy pink curtains and white sheets and collections of soft, colorful stuffed animals on their beds. "Fluffy," he said.

The dog had been sleeping with his head on his paws. When he heard Sergeant Joyce say "Fluffy," he lifted up his head and looked directly at him.

"Fluffy," Sergeant Joyce said again. The dog got to his feet and came over. "He likes the name," he told the team. "That's what I'm going to call him."

The men groaned and complained that no one would be afraid of a dog with a silly name like Fluffy. It was not a good argument, though. All of them had been impressed by how angrily the dog went for Iraqis, how alert he was to anyone approaching their compound, and how scared the local people seemed to be of him. He had been steadily gaining weight, but he would never be a really big dog. Yet to the locals, he was a giant.

Special Forces units are typically composed of relatively small groups of highly trained personnel who are equipped with special equipment and arms, and who operate under the principles of self-sufficiency, stealth, speed, and close teamwork. Special Forces train indigenous forces to fight guerrilla warfare. The public sometimes calls them "Green Berets" after their distinctive headgear and a song written about them during Vietnam.

The battle for Mosul ended on April 11, 2003, two days after the fall of Baghdad. The pro-Hussein forces couldn't keep up a defense against the American military. They abandoned the city. Kurdish fighters took over and tried to bring order, but they were faced with looters and infighting between Arabs and Kurds. Special Forces had to come in again to replace them.

Eventually, Sergeant Joyce and his unit were ordered to move south. Fluffy went with them. Fluffy now automatically protected all the Americans, and he was devoted to his partner. Sergeant Joyce said, "I think he knew I was his best friend. And he was mine."

Sergeant Joyce was due to return to his home in South Carolina in a month. That was wonderful news. But he started to worry about what was going to happen to Fluffy. "I had trained him to hate Iraqis, so there was no way I could leave him with them. I started to think about taking him home with me."

On one of his weekly calls to his wife, Caroline, he told her he was thinking of bringing a dog home from Iraq. Caroline later recalled that conversation. "I said, 'Excuse me, I didn't hear you right. It sounded like you said you want to bring a dog home.'" But she never once thought of asking her husband not to do it. Having him home meant so much to her and the girls. If he wanted to bring a dog, fine, bring a dog. Just come home in one piece, she prayed.

Sergeant Joyce sought out Air Force dog handlers from the 506th K-9 unit who had been trained at Lackland Air Force Base in San Antonio, Texas, where all military handlers and K-9s are trained. They were impressed with the story of Fluffy, and the rapid progress he'd made, but as usual, they groaned when he told them the dog's name. The handlers were sympathetic to his desire to take Fluffy home with him, but they told him that in past wars the U.S. military had not been very helpful to handlers who wanted to keep their dogs. Five thousand dogs served with their handlers in Vietnam, they told him, and many of the handlers asked to adopt the dogs at the end of the war. But as American troops rushed to evacuate the country, the military discarded the dogs. They gave some to the South Vietnamese army and some to anyone who wanted one. Some were euthanized. The rest were simply abandoned.

The story made Sergeant Joyce feel ill.

But one handler told him that those Vietnam veteran dog handlers had worked for years to get a law passed allowing handlers or qualified people to adopt retired Military War Dogs. The law passed in 2000. If he could somehow get Fluffy certified as a Military Working Dog, that law would cover him.[*]

That gave Sergeant Joyce hope. He set about on a mission to have Fluffy named as a U.S. Military War Dog. Since Fluffy had enlisted on the battlefield, it was complicated. But word of Fluffy and his work to protect his unit had spread throughout the region. And Sergeant Joyce was a persuasive advocate. The red tape of the military tends to slow things down, but through persistence and the cooperative attitude of many people, Sergeant Joyce was finally able to get it done. His Commanding Officer made Fluffy official and gave him orders to take the dog home. Sergeant Joyce told Fluffy, "You are now officially a soldier in Uncle Sam's Army."

The matter of getting Fluffy permission to enter the United States was just as complicated. But army veterinarians examined Fluffy and pronounced him fit and free from communicable disease. Sergeant Joyce needed a lot of official signatures, but when the big day arrived, he had them. On his way he stopped to say good-bye to the Air Force kennel master; the kennels were right at the airport, so it was convenient to stop by as he was leaving.

It was when they went to board the plane that the trouble began. Sergeant Joyce showed his thick cache of signed papers saying he could take the dog with him. But the Air Force pilot was

[*] Web site of the Military Working Dog Foundation, Inc.; www.militaryworkingdog.com.

not convinced. It was a very unusual request. He refused to let the dog board the C-17 Globemaster for the trip home. He told Sergeant Joyce he had seventeen minutes to get rid of the dog. The plane was taking off.

The pair scrambled back to the kennel master. Sergeant Joyce pleaded with him to hold Fluffy until the red tape could be worked out again. The kennel master was sympathetic but said he couldn't help him. He was expecting a new K-9 in three days. Now Sergeant Joyce was desperate. He said to the kennel master, "I put my life in his hands every day. And he put his in mine. I can't just abandon him."

The kennel master relented. "I can keep him for seventy-two hours," he said. "That's all."

"I'll get him by then," Sergeant Joyce promised.

"Wait, I'll give you the number of somebody who might be able to help you," he said hurriedly, because Sergeant Joyce was looking nervously out the window where the big jet's engine whine had shifted to a louder level. He scribbled a name and phone number on a piece of notepaper. Sergeant Joyce shoved it in his pocket and ran for the plane.

On the ride home, Sergeant Joyce held his head in his hands. It should have been a joyful moment. He was on home leave, and he'd soon be with his wife and daughters. But he couldn't stop thinking about Fluffy. He was scared for his dog—he felt that Fluffy was his partner and he'd let him down. Fluffy had worked hard to keep the unit safe, and now he was left behind.

The plane touched down in South Carolina at three a.m. Caroline and the two girls were waiting. Those were ecstatic moments. They were a close family, and had missed each other very much. The girls wanted to see the new dog that their father said had saved his life many times. They weren't sure they wanted a big dog in the house, but they did want to thank Fluffy for bringing their father back safely. Their dad had to tell them that because of red tape, Fluffy had been forced to stay behind. But we'll get him over here, he promised once again. "I'm going to fight for him."

⌒

IT WAS MOTHER'S DAY, May 11, 2003. At their home in Burlington, New Jersey, Ron Aiello's wife had one wish; that her husband and son would help her get her backyard garden into shape. There was weeding and fertilizing and planting to be done. The two men agreed to help.

The phone in the Aiello household rang at nine a.m. Ron answered to hear a polite, but nervous voice asking if he had a moment to talk about a soldier's war dog, which was currently stuck in Iraq. That grabbed Ron's interest right away. He asked the stranger how he could help.

⌒

IN 1964, WHEN Ron Aiello was only nineteen, he enlisted to serve in the United States Marine Corps. He liked the military life, but he missed the 130-pound German Shepherd he'd left at home. He found a solution for that. He signed up to train as a dog handler. Ron was assigned an eighteenth-month-old female German Shepherd named Stormy. They trained day and night for three months, and then shipped out to Vietnam.

"They matched up our personality with the dog's," Aiello said. "It worked out really well. It was the beginning of a beautiful friendship and the experience of a lifetime."

Their first patrol together in Vietnam was a defining moment in Ron's life. He remembers it clearly, even though forty years have passed.

Ron and Stormy were sent out to lead a platoon whose mission was to search two villages. The army suspected that Viet Cong had infiltrated the areas. Ron and Stormy's job was to ensure there were no ambushes lying in wait, and to steer the platoon away from any booby traps..

Soldier and dog entered the first village. Ron gave Stormy the order to search. They went from hut to hut and sniffed around any potential hiding places. Stormy looked at Ron, awaiting her next command. She had found nothing dangerous.

"I walked out and gave the "All clear" to the squad behind me," Ron said.

Later hey moved towards the second village, with Stormy six feet ahead of Ron. As they headed down a trail and into a clearing, Stormy suddenly stopped, her head snapping to attention, her eyes focused on a tree up ahead. She was alerting, but to what? Aiello knelt down beside her.

"Just as I knelt down, a sniper shot whizzed by my head," said Aiello. "If I had been standing up, it would have killed me."

Instead, Aiello alerted the thirty Marines behind him and dived behind a ridge while they fought. "That was my first time out, and everything we were trained to do worked," Aiello said. He is still proud and in awe of Stormy's ability, nearly half a century later. "She alerted me to the danger. I read the alert and we got out."

After that, Ron and Stormy often led patrols through the country. While the dog was with them, the soldiers never walked into an ambush and never stepped on a tripwire, as had happened so many times before. She provided a level of safety that was very welcome in a dangerous situation. Ron thinks her keen hearing could hear the click of a rifle from far away.

Stormy and the other dogs worked flawlessly. They alerted the American troops to booby traps, helped capture the enemy and even discovered a series of tunnels used by the Viet Cong that a demolition crew destroyed. Another time, Aiello and Stormy led a mission to flush enemy soldiers into a blockade that was being set up ahead. Back at the base camp in Da Nang, Aiello found out that he and Stormy had helped push an entire North Vietnamese platoon into the blockade, where they were captured and taken prisoner.

"Everybody was congratulating us. They even gave us better living quarters after that," Aiello said.

Ron was in Vietnam at the start of the American buildup of troops in 1965. He observed that at first, a lot of soldiers didn't want the dog on their team, thinking he would be a lot of trouble.

"That's until they found out how the dog could save their lives," Ron remembered. "Once they saw a dog stop a team and point out an ambush up ahead, they were won over. After that, they asked for the dog every time they went out."

The Vietnam conflict involved many military elements. Part of it was massive aerial bombing and large-scale conventional battles in the cities. The war the dog teams fought involved thousands of clashes between small units patrolling the mountains and jungles. The National Front for the Liberation of South Vietnam guerillas were able to control the pace of the fighting because they were familiar with the terrain and could disappear suddenly. Also, American troops could not tell friend from foe. Control over part of the population gave the guerrillas access to manpower, intelligence and financial resources. But they didn't have dogs, mostly due to a cultural dislike of all canines. The dog couldn't tell friend from foe, either, but he could tell you if someone was sneaking up on you. He could let you know your life was in danger in time for you to do something about it.

They were also invaluable on sentry duty at the bases. In World War II and Korea, soldiers had been able to reach secure rear areas in which to get rest and relaxation (R'n'R). In Vietnam, American troops were vulnerable to attack everywhere they went. Dogs were needed to patrol every facility and installation. The dog teams were heavily used. The number of American dogs serving in Vietnam grew to 5,000.

While he was in Vietnam, Ron experienced the tight bonding that develops between a soldier and his partner. Stormy saved his life many times. He also says she kept him sane.

"Part of the time, she was like a therapy dog," he said. "When I was with my dog, it cheered me up. Even when I was in a bad situation, I had my dog by my side. She kept the other Marines sane, too. She reminded everybody of the dog they had back home."

He spoke of Stormy as his dog, but she didn't belong to him. She was a valuable asset to the military. When Aiello left Vietnam thirteen months later, Stormy stayed behind and was assigned to work with another handler. It was one of the most difficult separations Ron had ever faced. He thought about her often, and tried to get news of her. He heard she'd worked with another handler from when he left in 1967 to 1970. But after that, he lost track of her.

He wrote to the Marines, explaining that he would like to adopt Stormy at the end of her service. He never heard back. When Saigon fell and U.S. troops performed a fast evacuation, he wrote again asking about Stormy. He imagined her in a kennel on a military base somewhere. He hoped she was loved and well cared for. But no one in the military wrote back.

"I suspected then that something was wrong," he said. "But I didn't know what. I had no idea they had just abandoned those dogs." He chokes up and has to clear his throat.

Being a Vietnam vet was tough in those days. It was an unpopular war. Returning soldiers were not greeted as heroes. They were treated with contempt and derision, as if it was their fault America had gotten into a losing war. Former soldiers couldn't find many people who wanted to hear about their experiences. Even though they'd been close friends in Vietnam, the dog handlers came home and lost touch with each other.

In the early 1990s, Ron bumped into an old dog handler friend and they started talking about their war days. They got in touch with another friend, and then another. It turned out that all the dog handler veterans had held on to their good memories. They missed the intense bonding they'd experienced in the war zone. And none of them had forgotten about their dogs. Like Ron, many of them had written, asking to adopt the war dogs. Like Ron, no one got an answer.

In 1993, a journalist got the idea to follow Ron in his quest to discover what Stormy's life had been like after he left her. The Freedom of Information Act meant it was now possible to get hold of military paperwork that had previously been unobtainable. Following a paper trail, Ron discovered that Stormy had had four handlers after him. When he tracked them down, all had wonderful memories. Every handler told him that Stormy had saved his life many times. When she searched vehicles at checkpoints, she found the weapons every single time. "I never had a false alert," Ron says. "She was right 100 percent of the time."

Following leads, Ron eventually found the name of the last kennel master to serve in Saigon as the war effort collapsed in 1973. It thrilled Ron to call him; now he'd find out, after all these years, where Stormy had been sent, and where she served her final days. That was the information he expected to obtain. What he got was something quite different.

In 1971, he learned, the military rounded up 1,000 of their war dogs and gave them to the South Vietnamese army.

Ron was shocked. "They didn't want those dogs for their military," Ron says. "One of our dogs weighed about 90 pounds, and a Vietnamese handler would have weighed 89. They were too small to control the dogs."

That wasn't all. Just before the fall of Saigon, knowing they were going to be leaving the country, the U.S. did it again, rounding up another 1,000 dogs and making a gift of them to the South Vietnamese army. Then, they euthanized many of the others. They gave dogs to any Vietnamese who wanted one. In the end, only 200 of the 5,000 military war dogs who served the United States in the war were brought home.

"You know what's so ironic? The Vietnamese *hated* dogs. It wasn't part of their culture. They wouldn't go near a dog. When they got a dog, they killed it and ate it. Dog meat was considered a great delicacy."

"They took home just a token few," Ron says sadly, "so they could say they didn't leave all the dogs."

Ron's beloved Stormy, the dog who had saved his life, who had given him her love and devotion for three years, and had served nobly and without complaint by his side day after day —had been left behind. And not just left behind. She had either been killed or eaten.

"I figure most of our five thousand dogs ended up—eaten. They gave us years of honorable service, and that's what we gave them.

"There were about 300 killed in action. Probably about 100 died of natural causes. That means somewhere around five thousand dogs were left, as if they were no more than a jeep or rifle. 'Here, take this, we don't need it anymore.'" Ron chokes up when he talks about it.

Ron shared the news with other handlers, all of who had always been eager to hear what had happened to their canine partners. All the men felt sick when they heard. "I never cried so hard in my life," one veteran said.

Ron's search put another document in his hands, one he wished he'd never seen. It was dated 1966, and it stated that none of the Military War Dogs would leave Vietnam. "That was the early part of the war, and they were already planning to abandon them," Ron says. "A lot of these dogs had been people's pets.

People had donated their dogs to the war effort. If people in the States had heard that we were going to abandon all these canines, people would have been up in arms."

Ron says that while they were in Vietnam, "they made us think that when the war was over, the dogs would come back to the States." Ron discovered that many handlers had asked to adopt their K-9s after the war, but were given all kinds of excuses. "They said, 'The dogs are too aggressive.' Well, they were aggressive, but they could have been used at other bases around the world, or back in the States. The ones who weren't so aggressive could have been retrained into civilian lives."

Some of the handlers were told the dogs weren't brought home because they had a blood disorder. That was true, Ron says. Some of them had picked up ehrlichiosis, which is carried by ticks."

"But we found out this was a common problem in the southern States, and easily treated by antibiotics. It was just another excuse."

"The military made the final decision on what was done with the dogs. They probably knew it was a terrible thing to do. And since it was an unpopular war, they wanted to sweep all the unpleasant incidents under the rug."

Paramus police Officer Al Gundersen was an air force dog handler in Vietnam. When he found out what happened to the dogs, he was upset. "These dogs put it on the line every day in Vietnam, and they were left there like an old Jeep," Gundersen said. "That wall in Washington would be twice as long if it weren't for those dogs."

The facts about Stormy festered in Ron's brain from 1993 to an inauspicious moment in 1999, when one of his old buddies called excitedly to say that a reunion was being planned. It was just for dog handlers, and it was going to be in Ocean City, Maryland. "Five of us drove down together. We walked in the hotel meeting room, and there were all these old guys sitting around. Turned out, this was a meeting of *World War* II dog handlers." Ron laughs. "We stayed anyway, and we all got along great. It was like we'd known each other all our lives."

Clearly, the Vietnam dog handlers needed an organization of their own, so those few men, with the leadership of Ron Aiello, formed The United States War Dogs Association, Inc. It's a non-profit organization of former and current U.S. Military Dog Handlers and supporting members, "committed to promoting the long history of the Military Service Dogs, establishing permanent War Dog Memorials, and educating the public about the invaluable service of these canines to our country."

The first year, the men put together an exhibit about their dogs, and set it up at dog shows. "The public interest was incredible," Ron says.

The club felt strongly that a monument to the service of the 5,000 Vietnam K-9s was needed. They began fundraising efforts. The club gained steam as more and more Vietnam dog handlers found out and joined.

So when Sergeant Russell Joyce called Ron and said he needed help bringing home his war dog, he was talking to the right person. "I don't want him to just be destroyed," Russell said. "Is there any way you can help me to bring him home?"

RON PROMISED RUSSELL he would do what he could. "What I heard in his voice was something I had heard hundreds of times from former military handlers. That intense bond handlers have with the dogs who work with them. That love and devotion. The Vietnam-era handlers still talk about their dogs to this day," Ron said. "Russell had that same emotion about Fluffy."

Ron had hope because he had an organization of men behind him who he knew would support the effort. His wife called out to him from the garden, but when he explained Russell's plight to her, she understood why he couldn't waste any time planting flowers.

Ron wrote two letters. The first was to Secretary of Defense Donald Rumsfeld.

"I told him, 'We did a bad thing in Vietnam. Let's not make the same mistake. Maybe we can make up for it a little by bringing this dog back.'"

The second letter went out to all the Vietnam veteran dog handlers. All knew that their dogs had been left behind to die in Vietnam. The plight of Sergeant Joyce and Fluffy struck a nerve that had been aching for years. Now, finally, there was a cause into which they could pour their energy, and maybe turn back the hopelessness and despair they'd felt for so long over the loss of their dogs. Each vet began his own campaign to bring Fluffy back. They called and wrote their senators and congressmen and people involved in Search and Rescue dog teams and animal rescue in every city and town. The Vietnam dog handlers, who were powerless to rescue their own wartime companions, mobilized to save Fluffy.

Joyce wrote:

> To whom it may concern:
> I'm in 3rd group Special Forces out of Fort Bragg, NC. I have just returned from Iraq today. While in Iraq, my team requested a dog for operational purposes. The Kurds brought us a German Shepherd breed that had obviously been abused and neglected by the Iraqi military. I became the handler for this dog and grew very attached to him. This dog was used in many combat operations in Northern Iraq and proved to be a wonderful "soldier." It was my team that took control over the

mountain north of Mosul (Maclube mountain). Anyway, I obtained all of the proper paperwork to have the dog shipped to the US so that I could adopt it but at the last minute there was some problem with politics. The dog meets all requirements to be shipped to the US. I only have 72 hours to find some way to get the dog released for travel and cut through this red tape or the dog will be destroyed. I have personally trained this dog for special military use and now the dog does not like Kurds or Iraqi persons, therefore, they will not be able to handle him.

All I need is some help in getting this animal here to the States, I will handle all of the expenses that it takes to get him here. I have a copy of all medical records, vaccinations, and orders for the dog. I can send a copy of this paperwork to anyone that can help me. I am a prior Ranger and currently a Special Forces soldier and our motto is "Never leave a fallen comrade." The military asked for this dog to serve, this dog lived through 2 shootings, mine fields, and all military actions in the North. Now, they are ready to discard him. I can't let that happen and I'm hoping that he can live his retirement with me here in the US. Please contact me if you can help or know of anyone who can. My 72 hours started on May 11 at 12 noon.

Thank you again,

SFC Russell W. Joyce

Fort Bragg, NC

Although not intended for distribution, this private e-mail found its way into wide distribution on the Internet. Sergeant Joyce recalls, "I had no idea that I'd woken a sleeping giant, the Vietnam dog handlers. They got in touch with *everybody* in Washington to get them in on this effort." Sergeant Joyce says that within a few days, he had 1,500 e-mails in his account, all of them committed to bringing Fluffy home.

It was normal to get phone calls from family and friends, welcoming him with relief that he'd returned safely. But now, when the phone rang, it was often a senator or congressman who was promising to do what he could to bring Fluffy home. The Joyces were overwhelmed with messages of support.

Ron Aiello says, "I hoped to get some correspondence from the Pentagon in about two weeks. I figured that's how long it would take. But the Pentagon called me *two days* later. They said, 'There are formalities we are going to have to take care of, but we'll do it. We are as committed to bring this dog home as you are.'"

When Ron expressed gratitude that they'd acted so quickly, the official on the phone said, "We've already been called by twenty-four senators." Secretary of the Defense Donald Rumsfeld was being swamped by personal calls from Capitol Hill; so many that he couldn't get any other work done. That was the power of the Vietnam vets, each one acting on his own across the country.

A lawyer who was at the Department of Defense recalled, "The Secretary came out and said, 'I want that dog brought home *now*. And if you can't do it, go get me some better lawyers.'"

While Sergeant Joyce waited anxiously at Fort Bragg, handlers at the 506th ESFS Air Force Squadron at Kirkuk Air Base were ordered to take care of Fluffy and forget about the 72-hour deadline. He was taken to a Military War Dog unit, where he received 24-hour, round-the-clock care. At last, he was safe.

The Defense Department kept their promise and worked on the matter as quickly as they could. Signatures from thirty people in the military hierarchy and numerous Department of Agriculture permits were needed to sign off on the transfer. The Pentagon people tracked them down. Agencies from the Department of Defense, Army, Air Force, and the consultant to the Army Surgeon General for Veterinary Clinical Medicine hustled to expedite Fluffy's retirement.

Don Stump, who was a U.S. army deputy division chief in

Washington, D.C., at the time, explained why. "It stirred me up when I thought about the selfless action and courage of Fluffy," Stump said.

Twenty days after he'd left Fluffy in Iraq, Sergeant Joyce was waiting for another C-17 to land. The Vietnam dog handlers waited anxiously across the country for Ron Aiello to tell them that Fluffy was home. And then, another heartbreaking delay.

"The kennel master called me from the airport in Iraq where the plane with Fluffy aboard was about to take off. He was screaming, 'We're under fire, we can't send him!'" Ron recalled. "A gun battle had broken out on the airfield. They had to postpone the flight. All the soldiers knew the Fluffy story, and that he was in that plane, headed for the states. They won that fight pretty quickly. Two hours later, the kennel master called back, relieved. He said, 'He's on the plane!'"

Ron quickly posted the news to vets around the country who were waiting to hear what happened. Many had despaired when they heard about the firefight. Bringing Fluffy home meant a lot to every one of them; and they had fought to get Fluffy on that plane.

Good-natured U.S. Air Force Major Jim Pompano, 615th Air Mobility Squadron, was on his way home to Travis Air Force Base in California, and scheduled to be on the same C-17. When he heard about Fluffy, he volunteered to be his escort.

As news of Fluffy's travel came in, from Sergeant Joyce and other military sources, Ron Aiello sent out a sequence of e-mails to the veteran dog handlers, giving a blow-by-blow description as events unfurled. At first, they were told that Fluffy would have to be sent to Lackland Air Force Base to be inspected and decommissioned before Sergeant Joyce could see him. That didn't worry the dog handlers. At least he would be safe in the United States. They were hanging on every word of Ron's e-mails. One of the final ones reads:

5/31/03 Fluffy is on plane heading to AFB in SC.
From: Ron Aiello
Sent: Sat May 31, 2003 4:28 pm
Subject: NEW UPDATE
Everything has changed. SFC Russell Joyce is at this time
waiting at the CHARLESTON AFB, SC for Fluffy's plane to land,
which should be in 30 minutes, 5PM, Sat. May 31, 3002. Fluffy
is almost here.

The final e-mail reads:

5/31/03 Fluffy Is Home with the Joyce's.
From: Ron Aiello
Sent: May 31, 2003 10:45 PM
Subject: Great News of an Update:
The Joyce family are all together now. SFC Joyce and Fluffy
have arrived home safely and I can tell you they are both very
happy to be together again. Bless them both.

The reunion took place May 31 on the flight line at Charleston
Air Force Base in South Carolina. In photos taken by Air Force
Print News, Fluffy is dragging Major Pompano across the airstrip
towards the one human he loves more than anyone else in the
world. A remarkably dry-eyed Sergeant Joyce, handsome in his
beige linen jacket, walks toward him and takes the leash, then
drops down to put an arm over Fluffy's shoulders.

Major Pompano said that Fluffy did not care for the take-off
or landing, but he'd been okay on the long flight.

"I think that America as a whole had a big hand in this, and it's
really a gift from the United States to me and a gift to Fluffy to be
able to come home," Sergeant Joyce told the AFPN reporter. "This
dog worked hard for us. He walked guard with every American

soldier in our compound, all night long. He chased stray dogs away. He never ran at the sound of bullets, and we were safe because he was there."

Ron Aiello says, "It's hard to put a number on how many lives one alert can save."

The army footed the $274 to fly Fluffy to North Carolina. "Bringing Fluffy to the States wasn't about me," Sergeant Joyce says. "It was about all the men who wept on the phone while they talked about the relationship they had with the dogs who served with them in war."

Ron Aiello is philosophical when he considers why the men in his organization campaigned so hard to get Fluffy home. " [The dogs] served with us, just as hard, just as loyal. And we betrayed them. We left them behind. We weren't going to let it happen again. We were going to get this one home. Like I wrote to Donald Rumsfeld, 'If we bring this dog home, it's kind of like a living memorial to the dogs who served in Vietnam.'"

Fluffy had a new job now: to adjust to quiet family life in a sunny suburb of Fayetteville, North Carolina. Russell Joyce was pretty nervous about whether or not Fluffy could do it.

Even years later, Sergeant Joyce maintains a careful eye over Fluffy. "He's not a pet," he says. "He's a trained military dog. We have to make a lot of adjustments in our home that people with a normal pet don't have. Before we open a door, we have to make sure about where he is so he doesn't run out. The girls can't have friends over, because we can't have a lot of kids making a lot of noise around him."

His daughter Elise, who was six, remembered, "At first, I didn't want Fluffy here because I thought I'd be afraid of him. My dad was always telling us he wasn't a pet and we weren't going to play with him."

Daughter Samantha, who was eleven, says, "Dad kept telling us, 'Don't let him out in the backyard. Don't run past him. Don't make any sudden movements.' But as soon as he got here, he started playing with us."

Despite all those cautions, when you look at Fluffy romping in the backyard with Elise and Samantha, you see a pet. When you see him pulling Sergeant Joyce down the street on his roller blades while the two girls ride bikes beside them, he sure looks like a pet. Caroline Joyce says, "He just walks beside my husband and gazes at him all the time. But he loves the girls. He wants to protect all of us. I'm happy we have him here, with Russ away so often. He makes us feel safe."

"I don't label him as a pet," Sergeant Joyce says. "I label him as a buddy."

E-mails to Sgt Russell Joyce:

Angela—AF Italy
I am proud to say "I was stationed with that dog!"; while deployed to Kirkuk, as a member of the 506th Security Forces.

In the short time I got to spend with the lovable dog, he boosted my morale ten-fold. His presence brought me a sense of home (by reminding me of my own dog); and the sadness in his eyes and scars on his body from the cruelty, served as a reminder as to why we were there.

Although I was saddened the day he left, I was happy to hear he was on his way to the States and would be taken care of. Actually, I contemplated trying to smuggle him out on my own if he didn't get the clearance. (Shhh!) Well, keep taking good care of Fluffy, and give the little guy (who's not so little anymore) a rub behind the ears for me!

Steve T.—Florida
I was a Sentry dog handler in Vietnam and I am very happy to see a working dog make it into retirement! My dog's name was Sargeant, 25X1, and I still miss him very much.

Greg H.—Glastonbury, CT

I was an Army Dog Handler, 212th MP Co. (Prince M234)in Vietnam in 1969. I miss that beautiful dog til this very day...

Sgt. Greg M. 377th SPS K9—Bangkok, Thailand

I was in Vietnam 68–70 with the 377th SPS K9, Lobo was my dog. I owe my life to him many times over, but I would not take back one day on the line with him as it was a special time in my life. I have never had the same feelings as I did walking with my dog in Vietnam.

Tommy H.—Tennessee

I was an Air Police Sentry Dog Handler at Clark AFB in Philippines from 1965–67. Then to Da-Nang Air Base from 67-68. My Dog at Clark was ARNO and my dog at Danang was PRINCE. a large blonde and black saddle shepard. Anyone who remembers anything about my partners, please write.

David A. —From NSHS Class of '86

Russell, sometimes a man will make differences in this world in ways he could not have imagined and I'd like to tell you that I am very proud to know you. Thank you.

I'm also glad to hear that Fluffy is home now taking care of your family.

"People wrote calling me and Fluffy heroes, but we were not the heroes at all," wrote Sergeant Joyce. "It's the military dog handlers who serve and protect others. It's the search-and-rescue teams that find lost kids, or attempted to rescue survivors on September 11. Or the police K-9 teams who put their lives on the line to protect us. It's the men and women of the armed forces who leave their families to go off to foreign lands to free others. And, most of all, it's all the Vietnam War vets who never got to a welcome home and were forced to leave behind their dogs that saved so many American lives. These are the heroes."

Fluffy not only saved lives and helped hundreds of servicemen return home safely, the legacy of his return helped heal the psychic wounds of thousands of Vietnam-era dog handlers.

CHAPTER 15

WHEN THE DOGS GO MARCHING IN

PANAMA CITY LIES ALONG the coast of the Gulf of Mexico in the Florida Panhandle, midway between Tallahassee and Pensacola. It is home to a U.S. air force station, resort hotels, and 27 miles of one of the world's softest, most luscious white-sand beaches. The sun grants it a warm climate year-round.

It was also the longtime home of Ruth Resmondo and her husband, Bill. In the early 1990s, Bill became ill and had to be admitted to a nursing home for care. Husband and wife both knew that he wouldn't ever be coming home. Ruth wanted his last days to be happy. She visited every day. But she didn't fail to notice that he was happiest on the days she received a secret dispensation from the nurses for bringing the couple's white Toy Poodle, Lane.

The little dog showered affection on her husband and made him laugh, even on bad days. Ruth saw that the simple act of the dog sitting in an easy chair with her husband would relieve his suffering. He could truly relax.

Other residents of the nursing home would often ask her if they could pet the dog. Ruth always consented. Often, the patients would begin to tell her about their own dog. On most days, patients stayed pretty much to themselves. But on the days the Poodle visited, patients came around smiling and Bill made new friends.

After her husband died, the memory of how much their Poodle had brightened his time in the nursing home kept coming back to Ruth. She started to think a good idea would be to have a group who would visit the sick, one who would take along their own dogs. But she wasn't sure just how to get it started.

First, she called the Greater Panama City Dog Fanciers Association and asked for advice. She was given the phone number of Ruth Ward, a Yorkshire Terrier owner.

"I'd never been involved with pet therapy," Ruth Ward says. "I didn't know anything about it. But I'd just been reading an article in *Dog World* magazine, and I shared that with her. She [Ruth Resmondo] and I became very good friends."

During the spring of 1992, Ruth Resmondo convinced her church, Forest Park United Methodist, that a worthwhile mission would be to sponsor volunteers to visit the sick with their dogs. Then she gathered some paraphernalia together—walkers, wheelchairs, crutches, canes, and other things used by people with a physical disability—and started a class.

On most days, the church fellowship hall was the scene of Bible classes, pancake breakfasts, and senior get-togethers. But on Saturday afternoons, it was a therapy dog-training center. Six other people joined the two Ruths, making sure their dogs wouldn't become spooked by noisy wheelchairs, falling walkers, or other such events they might encounter in the nursing-home environment.

Ruth Resmondo thought of a good name, a new spin on the acronym, PAWS: Pets Are Working Saints. The name seemed to put into words how many of the members felt about their dogs.

Back then, the "therapy dog" concept was not well known. Most hospitals and medical centers were strictly off-limits for dogs. The group could find only two places willing to have them visit, Glen Cove Nursing Home and Panama Nursing Center. On the first day, the PAWS volunteers showed up with an assortment of big and small canines. An administrator met them at the front door and said to visit anyone who didn't appear to be afraid of the dogs.

The volunteers went from room to room, asking the patients if they would like to have a visit with the dogs. "If they wanted to hold them, we plunked them down right on the bed," Ruth Ward said.

Most of the people who were awake and alert were happy to have a PAWS visit. They were usually people who had had pets of their own. "We often heard, 'I had a Chihuahua, or some sort of dog, but I had to give it away' or 'My children have it.'"

Paws Are Working Saints began with six people and two nursing homes. From the first Sunday afternoon, the visits were a huge success. As word spread, more and more volunteers joined them with their pets.

"Shortly after we started, we got a cat, a bird, a pot-bellied pig, and a ferret. The pot-bellied pig was the hit. Everybody wanted to see her. We had a hard time getting out of the nursing home when we had the pig with us." Rosie the pig wore a harness and was very obedient, except that she wouldn't get into the elevator. She would go up and down steps just fine, but the elevator scared her. To a pig, it was just a small strange room that shook.

Ruth found that her own three dogs loved the PAWS visits. She and her husband made it part of their regular routine. "We would give the dogs a bath and say, 'It's PAWS day.' They knew exactly what we were talking about. They'd get excited and jump and bark and run around until we'd go."

From that small beginning in 1992, every health facility in Panama City asked to have "Saints" visits. The group went to hospitals, rehab centers, and homes for people with mental disabilities. They began to visit an after-school program for latchkey kids. It was mainly a social visit, but it gave the members a chance to educate children about dogs.

Ruth says that of the places they visit, her favorite is the veterans' home. "I somehow picture them as young soldiers who fought for our freedom. It warms my heart that I can contribute just a few minutes of pleasure to them."

Occasionally, a resident would refuse a pet visit, usually because they said they were allergic. Once, Ruth stepped into the room of a tall, thin woman and asked if she wanted to see the dogs. "She said, 'Nooooooooooo, I'm afraid!' On one visit I decided I wasn't going to take no for an answer anymore, so I turned the backside of my little Yorkie toward her and asked her, 'touch this end, this end doesn't bite.' She very gingerly reached out her hand and touched Ginger. She drew her hand back real quick. I said, 'See? She didn't hurt you.' Next thing you know, she's petting Ginger. She overcame her fear and decided dogs weren't so bad after all."

On another occasion, Ruth approached a woman sitting in a chair in her room and asked if she'd like to see the dogs. The woman turned toward her and said, "I can't see them." Ruth realized that she was blind, So she asked, "But would you like to feel them?" The woman gave a big smile, so she put her Yorkie, Sophie, in her lap. "When I asked her what the dog felt like she said, 'Silk,' which is exactly what a Yorkie should feel like."

Another woman asked Ruth to bring her the long, lustrous Yorkie hair that was left after grooming so she could make pincushions from it.

When Ruth and her husband retired, they made a lot of vacation trips around the country in their motor home. "We'd be gone for a while, and we'd come back and we'd go for a PAWS visit, and some of the patients we had known and gotten attached to had died. It was very difficult for us. In fact, there were times when I thought, I just can't go back. It was like you lost a member of your family. I had to tell myself: 'These people are old, and they're sick, and they're following the path God set for them. They're going to die. And if you're going to participate you've got to expect that. Just go and do whatever you can for them.'"

A local hospice program learned of the Working Saints and asked if some of the volunteers would visit with patients in hospice. The administrator warned that working in hospice care requires emotional strength, because the patients there are near death. That's where Ruth and her husband met the tall, thin gentleman she called "Jake the colonel."

When she entered Jake's room, Ruth saw a formerly robust man who had once stood six-foot-four. At 89, Jake could no longer walk. He buzzed around the nursing home in a motorized scooter.

"As soon as we met, Jake grabbed Sophie and held her. He was so comfortable with her that I could tell he had once had a Yorkie. It was like he had his own dog back. When it was time for us to leave, he said to her, 'I wish you didn't have to go—I wish you could stay with me.' It just broke my heart."

The next time she and Sophie visited, they found that the canine had inspired the colonel to tell a lot of the other patients about his life before hospice and the Yorkie who had shared it with him. He grinned when he saw them.

Ruth had to laugh. "The funny thing was, here's this full colonel with a little foo-foo dog in his lap, and he's going to show her off to his friends. He didn't care who thought what. He loved that dog. It was comical."

Part of the comedy came from Sophie's wild outfits. Ruth dressed Sophie in a different outfit for each visit. She would wear a little pink tweed coat with black piping and fur trim; some days, it was her red Mad Hatter's outfit. Ruth thought she looked adorable in her Little Bo Peep coat with its soft, curly wool. In the Ward household, there is an armoire filled with clothes for Sophie and the younger Yorkie, Missy. A black-and-silver New Year's dress, to celebrate the millennium; a turquoise dupioni silk coat with black sequins; a punk rock–type pink leather jacket; for more exotic moods, her Japanese kimono. There is even a clown outfit to create some circus atmosphere.

Ruth stops to count up all the outfits in Sophie's closet. There are 35. She laughs, knowing that it's all a little silly but loving the fun and extravagance and the smiles it brings to lonely patients.

They learned that Jake and his wife had brought their own Yorkie, Precious, with them when they first went into a nursing home. She kept them active even when they felt ill. But one day, Jake's wife stumbled and fell over the dog, injuring herself and causing extra work for the nurses and aides. Jake and his wife were told that Precious had to go. Their children found a home for Precious. But shortly after being taken away from them, Precious died. Not long after, Jake's wife died. Jake was alone now. He missed both of his beloved companions.

When people are signed into hospice, it is because they are believed to be within six months of death. But Jake's terminal cancer went into remission. Against the odds, he started to get better. Instead of six months, he was in hospice for five years.

One day, Ruth was on an errand when she realized she was near the nursing home, so she parked and headed in to say hello. Jake gave her a dressing down. "You don't go if you don't take Sophie. He liked us fine, but it was Sophie who perked up his day."

Ruth realized she just might as well reach for her car keys and Sophie in the same moment, because everyone in town expected to see her; the hairdressers, secretaries, drugstore clerks. Jane, Dr. Frooy's receptionist, kept Sophie on her lap while Ruth was being examined.

Just as she had done with Jake, Sophie had secured a place in the heart of the Panama City community.

Jake's mood had improved so much that he went on a field trip out to the airbase to watch the air show. It must have been exciting for him to return to the place where he'd spent so much of his life. He saw lean, handsome young men in their uniforms, just as he had been. But watching the acrobatics in the sky disoriented him; Jake ran his scooter off the sidewalk and it pitched over, coming down on top of him. He was hurt, but he never complained.

A few days later, Ruth was doing laundry when the phone in the kitchen rang. Sophie started to bark. It was a nurse from hospice. Jake had died. Ruth felt as though she'd lost one of her own family. That was the downside of this sort of volunteer work. They'd cared deeply for Jake for three years. Now they would miss him just as deeply.

When the Pets Are Working Saints group started out, they worried about finding enough time in their days for the visits. But they found that long visits were not necessary. "They don't want a lot of company for a long period of time. A quick, short visit gives them a little bright spot in their day. Occasionally, you'll find someone who wants you to sit and talk with them. But the ones who are bedridden only want to give you their attention for five or ten minutes."

Ruth had been thinking of getting a playmate for Sophie, one from her own species to give her a rest from all the work she did with human nursing-home patients. Ruth found out about a Yorkie named Missy, who had been returned to her original owner and was being fostered until a permanent home could be found for her. When Ruth asked for the address to pick up Missy, she was amused to learn it was her own daughter's, who like her mom was a soft touch for any Yorkie.

"Missy is a good nursing-home dog as long as we're with her. But because of her past history, she gets very anxious if we're out of her sight. She doesn't like travel. She wants to stay home where she feels secure. So before a PAWS trip, we give her a little Rescue Remedy. It takes about an hour and she settles down." Missy has a T-shirt that says, "I Have Issues."

Ruth says she believes fully in the healing power of dogs. Then she pauses for a moment, and her voice becomes filled with pain as she relates how she came to understand in a personal way how a little dog can help heal a life.

"We started off with a Schnauzer when our son died. He was only seventeen." She pauses to stroke the Yorkie on her lap, and her Brussels Griffon, sensing a change in her mood, wants to be held, too.

"I knew he was depressed and I did what I could to help him, in the ways you could help back in 1977. Today, if he were depressed, I'd have him off to the doctor in a minute. Then, there wasn't a lot known about depression and mental illness. No one had any idea of how bad he was feeling, and suddenly, he was gone. He committed suicide.

"I was totally shocked. We never dreamed anything like that would ever happen in our family. It was a very hard time."

At that unfortunate time Ruth's daughter was fourteen. The siblings had always gone back and forth to school together. The daughter now walked home alone to an empty house since both parents worked. She asked her mother for a dog.

Ruth and her husband bought the Miniature Schnauzer as her Christmas present that year. True to his breed, he was a faithful, intelligent dog who provided the company her daughter so badly needed. Ruth saw the warmth and comfort the little dog brought to their home and decided she needed a dog of her own. She chose a Yorkie. Upon returning from a dog show and seeing a Brussels Griffon, Ruth said, 'I've got to have one of those.'" Since then, the Ward household has always included two or three dogs.

After going through the most traumatic possible event in the life of a mother, Ruth found comfort and healing in the presence of her dogs. Many years later, she returned that gift by taking other dogs to visit the sick and bring them some of the same comfort and healing she had received. The circle was complete.

"I do not think that dogs have souls," she says, speaking strongly. "I never get into those discussions about going to the Rainbow Bridge and that sort of thing. [Some people believe in a bridge, "just this side of heaven," where you and your once deceased and now healthy pet will meet and then cross over together into heaven.] Every once in a while the humane society runs a story about a dog as if it's a human, 'Why am I here? My family put me here and all I wanted to do was love them.'

"I really don't think dogs are aware of that sort of thing. I think dogs know when people are good or bad." She relates the story of a friend's Yorkie, who taught himself to alert his owner to heart attacks.

"He has heart problems, and she's told him twice when he's in trouble. It's just something dogs sense. I have sleep apnea, which means my breathing stops occasionally. Lita comes over and gets excited until I wake up and start breathing again. She knows I'm having some kind of problem and she wants to help. I think it has to do with the bond you have with your dog. The dog knows you so well, she is aware of everything about your body chemistry."

On the second Sunday of October every year, Forest Park United Methodist Church holds a blessing of the PAWS ministry. All the animals are welcomed into the church. While the choir sings a special hymn, the PAWS volunteers march in procession with the "Working Saints" on leashes beside them.

Each animal and owner team is called by name to receive a Certificate of Blessing. It's signed by the pastor and has a little gold emblem of a paw print. On it is the Bible passage that the group uses as a motto: "But now ask the beasts and let them teach you." (Job 12:7). That passage continues,

> And the birds of the heavens, and let them tell you,
> Or speak to the earth, and let it teach you;
> And let the fish of the sea declare to you.
> Who among all these does not know
> That the hand of the Lord is here.

TO FIND OUT MORE

THE CHURCH OF ST. ROCH
24 rue Saint-Roch
Paris, 75001 France
Phone: (33) 01 42 44 13 20

PETS ARE WONDERFUL SUPPORT
645 Harrison St., Suite 100
San Francisco, CA 94107
Phone: 415.979.9550 Fax: 415.979.9269
www.pawssf.org
E-mail: info@pawssf.org

DELTA SOCIETY THERAPY
A national organization that provides training materials to local
        volunteers who want to get involved in therapy dog and
        animal-assisted therapy work. Delta Society's Pet Partners
        program provides information on how to screen and train
        volunteers and their pets for visiting animal programs in
        hospitals, nursing homes, rehabilitation centers, schools, and
        other facilities. Delta developed the standards of practice for
        therapy dogs, which provide guidance in animal selection,
        personnel training, and development of a treatment plan. Delta
        honors service and therapy dogs with annual national awards.
875 124th Ave. NE, Suite 101
Bellevue, WA 98005-2531
Phone: 425.679.5500 (8:30 A.M. to 4:30 P.M. PST, Monday–Friday)
        Fax: 425.679.5539
E-mail: info@deltasociety.org

ANGEL ON A LEASH

Angel On A Leash, a New York City–based therapy dog program, began
as a charity of the Westminster Kennel Club. Angel On A Leash
volunteer teams visit hospitals and rehabilitation centers such as
Morgan Stanley Children's Hospital and the Ronald McDonald House.
Angel On A Leash champions the use of therapy dogs in healthcare
facilities, schools, rehabilitation centers, hospice, extended care,
correctional facilities, and crisis intervention.

Greer Griffith, Program Coordinator gggreer4@mac.com

Phone: 212.488.8279

David Frei, President/CEO david@angelonaleash.com

Phone: 646.339.5577

THERAPY DOGS INTERNATIONAL, INC.

88 Bartley Rd., Flanders, NJ 07836

Phone: 973.252.9800 Fax: 973.252.7171

E-mail: tdi@gti.net, www.tdi-dog.org

CANINE COMPANIONS FOR INDEPENDENCE

P.O. Box 446

Santa Rosa, CA 95402-0446

Phone, nationwide: 800.572.BARK (800.572.2275)

Phone, Santa Rosa Headquarters: 866.CCI-DOGS (866.224.3647)

www.caninecompanions.org.

Photos from the graduation ceremony can be seen at: www.
caninecompanions.org/northeast/GraduationFeb2007.pdf.pdf

ASSISTANCE DOG INSTITUTE, the only university-level educational organization for training service dogs.

1215 Sebastopol Rd.

Santa Rosa, CA 95407

Phone: 707.545.DOGS (707.545.3647)

Fax: 707.545.0800

E-mail: info@ assistancedog.org

http://assistancedog.org/

ASSISTANCE DOGS INTERNATIONAL, national umbrella organization for assistance dog organizations

P.O. Box 5174

Santa Rosa, CA 95402

info@adionline.org
www.adionline.org

XOLOITZCUINTLE CLUB USA
www.xoloworld.com

X-CPR—XOLOS FOR CHRONIC PAIN RELIEF
c/o Nancy Gordon
PAWS FOR COMFORT
P.O. Box 601784
San Diego, CA 92160
Phone: 619.599.5228
Fax: 619.546.5458
www.pawsforcomfort.com

NATIONAL FIBROMYALGIA ASSOCIATION
www.fmaware.org

CFIDS ASSOCIATION (chronic fatigue and immunodeficiency
       Dysfunction syndrome)
www.cfids.org.

B-NOSES, LLC, Olfactory Consultants
Dr. James C. Walker, President
2736 Pecan Road
Tallahassee, FL 32303
Phone: 850.566.2462
jwalker@bnoses.com
THE NATIONAL CANCER INSTITUTE
U.S. National Institute of Health
www.cancer.gov

THE PINE STREET FOUNDATION
The Pine Street Foundation's mission is to help people with cancer reach
       more informed treatment decisions, through meta-analysis of global
       medical literature and the conduct of innovative clinical trials.
124 Pine St
San Anselmo, CA 94960-2674
Phone: 415.455.5878
www.pinestreetfoundation.org

THE EPILEPSY FOUNDATION
www.efa.org

SEIZURE DOG INFORMATION AND RESOURCES
www.adionline.org
www.iaadp.org
www.inch.com/~dogs/service.html
www.pawswithacause.org

CANINE ASSISTANTS
Jennifer Arnold, president
3160 Francis Road
Alpharetta, GA 30004
Phone: 770.664.7178
Toll Free Phone: 800.771.7221
Fax: 770.664.7820
www.canineassistants.org

U.S. WAR DOGS ASSOCIATION, INC.
Ron Aiello, President
ronaiello@uswardogs.org
1313 Mt. Holly Road
Burlingotn, NJ 08016
Phone: 609.747.3940
www.uswardogs.org

VIETNAM DOG HANDLERS ASSOCIATION
www.vdhaonline.org

SPACE COAST WAR DOG ASSOCIATION
PO Box 254315
Patrick AFB, FL 32925
admin@scwda.org
www.scwda.org

BIBLIOGRAPHY

BOOKS

American Rare Breed Association. *American Rare Breed Association Standards.*
  ARBA, 2006.

Anderson, R. K., Ben Hart, and Lynette Hart. *The Pet Connection: Its Influence
  on Our Health and Quality of Life.* University of Minnesota, 1984.

Andrews, Ted. *Animal Speak: The Spiritual & Magical Powers of Creatures Great &
  Small.* Llewellyn Publications, 1993.

Beck, Alan M. *Between Pets and People: The Importance of Animal Companionship.*
  Purdue University Press, 1996.

Becker, Dr. Marty, with Danelle Morton. *The Healing Power of Pets:
  Harnessing the Amazing Power of Pets to Make and Keep People Happy and Healthy.*
  Hyperion, 2002.

Bergin, Bonnie, and Sharon Hogan. *Teach Your Dog to Read.* Broadway,
  2006.

Bergin, Bonnie, and Robert Aquinas McNally. *Bonnie Bergin's Guide to
  Bringing Out the Best in Your Dog.* Little, Brown, 1995.

Brannigan, Cynthia A. *The Reign of the Greyhound.* Howell Book House,
  2004.

Burch, Mary R. *Wanted! Animal Volunteers.* Howell Book House, 2003.

Burnam, John. *A Soldier's Best Friend: Scout Dogs and Their Handlers in the
  Vietnam War.* Carroll & Graf, 2003.

———. *Dog Tags of Courage: Combat Infantrymen and War Dog Heroes in
  Vietnam.* Lost Coast Press, 2005.

Butler, Kris. *Therapy Dogs Today: Their Gifts, Our Obligation*. Funpuddle Publishing Associates, 2004.

Caras, Roger. *The Bond: People and Their Animals*. Simon & Schuster, 1997.

—————. *A Perfect Harmony: The Intertwining Lives of Humans and Animals throughout History*. Fireside, Simon & Schuster, 1996.

—————. *A Dog Is Listening: The Way Some of Our Closest Friends View Us*. Summit Books, 1992.

Clark, Anne Rogers, and Andrew H. Brace, eds. *The International Encyclopedia of Dogs*. Howell Book House, 1995.

Coppinger, Raymond, and Lorna Coppinger. *Dogs: A New Understanding of Canine Origin, Behavior, and Evolution*. Scribner, 2001.

Coren, Stanley. *The Intelligence of Dogs*. Free Press, 2005.

—————. *Why We Love the Dogs We Do*. Free Press, 1998.

Craige, Patricia. *Born to Win, Breed to Succeed*. Doral Publishing, 1997.

Crawford, Jacqueline J., and Karen A. Pomerinke. *Therapy Pets: The Animal-Human Healing Partnership*. Prometheus Books, 2003.

Denlinger, Milo G. *The Complete Dachshund*. Denlinger's, 1949.

Finem, Aubrey, ed. *Handbook on Animal-Assisted Therapy: Theoretical Foundations and Guidelines for Practice*. Academic Press, 2000.

Grandin, Temple. *Animals in Translation: Using the Mysteries of Autism to Decode Animal Behavior*. Scribner, 2005.

—————. *Genetics and the Behavior of Domestic Animals*. Academic Press, 1997.

—————. *Thinking in Pictures, and Other Reports from My Life with Autism*. Vintage, 1995.

Griffith, Beatrice Fox. *Historic Dogs: An Outline in Pictures of the Story of the Dog, from the Earliest Records to the Present Day*. Majestic Press, 1952.

Isabell, Jackie. *Genetics: An Introduction for Dog Breeders*. Alpine Blue Ribbon Books, 2003.

Jones, Arthur Frederick, and John Rendel. *The Treasury of Dogs*. A Ridge Press Book, Golden Press, 1964.

Knapp, Caroline. *Pack of Two: The Intricate Bond Between People and Dogs*. Delta, 1998.

Krause, Louise. *Heroes All Without Question*. FAST Publications, 2003.

Lingenfelter, Mike, and David Frei. *The Angel by My Side*. Hay House, 2003.

Miller, Constance. *Shining Dog, Shadowy Wolf.* Afghan Hound Club of America, 2001

———. *Gazehounds: Search for the Truth.* Hoflin Publishing, 1988.

Salotto, Pearl. *Pet-Assisted Therapy: A Loving Intervention and an Emerging Profession Leading to a Friendlier, Healthier, and More Peaceful World.* DJ Publications, 2001.

Sheldrake, Rupert. *Dogs That Know When Their Owners Are Coming Home and Other Unexplained Powers of Animals.* Crown Publishers, 1999.

Schoen, Allen M., DVM, MS. *Kindred Spirits: How the Remarkable Bond Between Humans & Animals Can Change the Way We Live.* Broadway Books, 2001.

White, Joseph J. *Ebony & White: The Story of the K-9 Corps.* Doral Publishing, 1996.

Wilson, Cindy C., and Dennis C. Turner, eds. *Companion Animals in Human Health.* Sage Publications, 1998.

PERIODICALS

Abrams, Sally. "The Power of Pets." *BJ's Journal* 2, no. 4 (1999).

Allen, Karen M. "Coping with Life Changes & Transitions: The Role of Pets." *Interactions,* 13 (1995): 5–8.

Anderson, W. P., and C. M. Reid, and G. L. Jennings. "Pet Ownership and Risk Factors for Cardiovascular Disease." *Medical Journal of Australia* 157 (1992): 298–301.

Barker, Sandra B. "Therapeutic Aspects of the Human-Companion Animal Interaction." *Psychiatric Times* 16, no. 2 (1999): 45–46.

Barker, Sandra B., and Kathryn S. Dawson. "The Effects of Animal-Assisted Therapy on Anxiety Ratings of Hospitalized Psychiatric Patients." *Psychiatric Services: A Journal of the American Psychiatric Association* 49 (June 1998): 797–801.

Brown, S. W., and V. Strong. "The Use of Seizure-Alert Dogs." *Seizure* 10 (2001): 39–41.

Caprilli, Simona, and Andrea Messeri. "Animal-Assisted Activity at A. Meyer Children's Hospital: A Pilot Study." *Evidence-based Complementary and Alternative Medicine* (June 1, 2006) (on-line).

Centers for Disease Control and Prevention Researchers (CDC). "New

Chronic Fatigue Syndrome Prevalence Rates." *Population Health Metrics* (8 June 2007) (on-line).

Cole, Kathie M., Anna Gawlinski, and Neil Steers. *"Scientific Measurements Document Therapeutic Dogs Lower Anxiety, Stress and Heart and Lung Pressure among Heart Failure Patients."* Study presented at the American Heart Association's Scientific Sessions in Dallas, Texas, in November 2005.

Fischman, J. "The Pet Prescription." *U.S. News & World Report,* 4 December 2005, 72–74,3p,3c.

Heimlich, Kathryn. "Animal-Assisted Therapy and the Severely Disabled Child: A Quantitative Study." *Journal of Rehabilitation* 67 (October/December, 2001): 48–54.

Hynes, Angela. "The Healing Power of Animals: People with Pets Have Reduced Levels of Stress, Depression, and Heart Risk." *Natural Health,* March 2005.

Gordon, Serena. "The Emotional Benefits of Pet Ownership Can Be Significant, More Social Contact, Lower Anxiety, Better Quality of Life." *Health Day News,* 17 January 2007.

Hart, Dr. Lynette. "The Healing Power of the Human-Animal Bond," "The Role of Pets in Enhancing Human Well-Being: Effects for Older People," and "Animal-Assisted Therapy for Children with Special Needs." *Newsletter of the American Association of Human-Animal Bond Veterinarians,* various issues (2000–2007).

Levinson, B. M., "Pets: A Special Technique in Child Psychotherapy." *Mental Hygiene* 48 (April 1964): 243–48.

Macauley, Beth L. "Animal-Assisted Therapy for Persons with Aphasia: A Pilot Study." *Journal of Rehabilitation Research & Development* 43 (May/June 2006): 357–66.

Provasi, Chiara. "The Value of Pet Therapy." *Project Coordinator, Multiple Sclerosis International Federation,* 5 (2005).

Reeves, William C. et al. "Prevalence of Chronic Fatigue Syndrome in Metropolitan, Urban, and Rural Georgia." *Population Health Metrics,* 5 June (2007) (on-line).

Roth, Joanne. "Pet Therapy Uses with Geriatric Adults." *International Journal of*

Psychosocial Rehabilitation (Dec. 1999) (University of La Verne).

Stevens, Karen Lee. "The Proof Is in the Petting: Animal Lovers Already Know This—But Research Confirms That Dogs Are Good for Our Health." *Dog Watch*, 1 (June 2006).

Strong V., et al. "Seizure-Alert Dogs — Fact or Fiction?" *Seizure* 8 (February 1999): 62–65.

Virues-Ortega, J., and G. J. Buela-Casal. "Psychophysiological Effects of Human-Animal Interaction: Theoretical Issues and Long-Term Interaction Effects." *The Journal of Nervous and Mental Disease* 194 (January 2006): 52–57.

Warwick, P., et al. "Pet Ownership and Risk Factors for Cardiovascular Disease." *Medical Journal Australia* 157 (1992): 298–301.

Mizutani, Wataru. *"Difference in Social Communication among Elderly People : Animal Present Situation Vs. Animal Non-Present Situation."* (Japanese Animal Hospital Association) Report to 11th Annual Conference on Human-Animal Interactions, Tokyo, August 2007.

Wells, Deborah. "Domestic Dogs and Human Health: An Overview." *British Journal of Health Psychology* 12, no. 1 (2007): 145–56.

Williams H., and A. Pembroke. "Sniffer Dogs in the Melanoma Clinic?" A letter in *Lancet*. 1(1989): 734.

ONLINE

Assistance Dog Institute, www.assistancedog.org

Allen, Karen, 2005. Coping with Life Changes & Transitions: The Role of the Pet. Delta Society, Online. www.deltasociety.org/ AnimalsHealthGeneralCoping.htm - 31k

Pet Therapy, Holisticonline.com

The Benefits We Experience When Pets (Animals) Are Beside Us, www.holisticonline.com

Ptak, Andrea Leigh, 2005. *Studies of Loneliness: Recent Research into the Effects of Companion Animals on Lonely People.* Delta Society, the Human Animal Health Connection Web site at http://www.deltasociety.org/Animals HealthGeneralLoneliness2.htm. First published *Interactions* 13 (1998): 7.

Canine Companions for Independence, www.cci.org

The Official Fluffy Web site, www.k9fluffy.com

International Association of Assistance Dog Partners, www.iaadp.org

K9 History: Dogs in War and Peace, http://community-2.webtv.net/Hahn-
    50thAP-K9/K9History/index.html

K9 Hero.com, www.k9hero.com

Military Working Dog Foundation, www.militaryworkingdogs.com

United States War Dog Association, www.uswardogs.org

Vietnam Dog Handler Association, www.vdhaonline.org

Vietnam Military Police Sentry Dog Alumni, www.sdalumni.ctshosting.com

Prison Pet Partnership Program, www.prisonpetpartnership.org

TELEVISION AND VIDEO

Amazing Pets, weekly program, Animal Planet Cable Network

Science of Dogs, National Geographic Channel

PBS, *Nature*: Dogs That Changed the World

PBS, *Nature*: Extraordinary Dogs

PBS, *Nature*: Dogs: The Early Years

PBS, *Nature*: A Second Chance: Prisoner Pet Partnership Programs

PBS, *Nature*: Dogs and More Dogs

Australian Broadcasting Corporation, *The Animal Attraction: Human Being's Best
    Friends*

INDEX

D

ACKNOWLEDGMENTS

MANY PEOPLE ASSISTED me in completing this manuscript. My heartfelt thanks go out to each and everyone, to those who made introductions and those who patiently explained everything I didn't understand.

Thanks to Nancy Bennett for theories of evolution, wolves, and the Nth generation, and to Peter San Paolo, for his expertise in ecclesiastical matters. Thanks to Nancy Gordon, for sharing her fascination with Xolos. My deep appreciation to Russie McDerment-Fogarty, Jean and Amber Mendres, Cara Pelligrini, Don Hancock, Carol Vogel, and Josh Caporale for stories of their bonds with their dogs.

Pets Are Wonderful Support do a great job of keeping very ill San Franciscans together with their pets. PAWS is a truly unique organization. Thanks go to John Lipp, Prado Gomez, Andrea Brooks and Randy Allgaier and Dr. Lynette Hart of the University of California/Davis School of Veterinary Medicine.

At the Assistance Dog Institute, Bonnie Bergin, Rick Yount, and Jorjan Powers clarified the history and current breeding and training of service dogs. At Canine Companions for Independence, Dina Ghram and all the staff of the Eastern Regional office and Puppy Raiser extraordinaire

Wendi Hartman shed light on the experience of raising a dog to be of service.

Many thanks to Dr. James C. Walker of Tallahassee for being such a great instructor of the intricacies of the canine olfactory system. Kudos to co-founders of the Pine Street Clinic, Dr. Michael McCulloch and Dr. Michael Bronfman, whose truly groundbreaking work in finding cures for cancer reaches so many people.

For teaching me about the magical world of dogs who can alert to the onset of seizures, Fran Atkins, Sandy Barnett, and Mitch Peterson. For being pioneers in the training of such dogs, Dana Babb of the Paws-Abilities Dog Training Center in Tukwila, Washington, and Jennifer Arnold of Canine Assistants in Alpharetta, Georgia.

In the field of military dogs: thanks first go to Ron Aiello and all the members of the United States War Dog Association. The Vietnam veteran military dog handlers are responsible for changing the law so that dogs will no longer be left behind, and so that elderly K-9s are no longer destroyed, but can be adopted into loving homes. Sergeant First Class Russell Joyce and his wife, Caroline Joyce, were generous with their time and explanations, even though Sergeant Joyce is far too modest. If I made Fluffy and Sergeant Joyce sound like heroes, it was over his strong objections, as he has never failed to insist that the real heroes are the K-9 handlers of the U.S. military, past and present. From Lackland Air Force Base, Public Affairs Officer Oscar Balladares supplied detailed information about military dogs and their lives.

Therapy Dogs: Thank you to David Frei, Greer Griffith, and Gay Cropper of Angel On A Leash in New York. Blessings to Ruth Ward and all the Pets Are Working Saints of Panama City. They are truly ones who love their fellow man. May your tribe increase.

My veterinarian Dr. Peter Batts, my wonderful brothers, John and Drew, my first mentor, Mrs. Franklin Koehler of Merrybrook Kennels and my first mentor in Whippets, Jean Balint of Wyndsor

Kennels. Thanks to Max Magder, Gini Sikes, and Liz Williams for general inspiration and guidance.

My editor, Richard Fumosa, brought welcome details of St. Rocco in Venice and New Orleans and helped with Aztec history in addition to his editing duties. Thanks also go to Alyson Books publisher Dale Cunningham; without her idea there would be no book.